The Human Factor

Volume 2

Re-capturing
The Meaning Of Existence For Your Life

Paa Kwasi Mfoamfo

Why Am I Here?

The Loss Human Factor, Volume 2

Paa Kwasi Mfoamfo

Published by Paa Kwasi Mfoamfo, 2024.

Table of Contents

"Why Am I Here?"

———

The Loss Human Factor

Volume 2

———

Re-Capturing

The Meaning Of Existence For Your Life

Paa Kwasi Mfoamfo

Dedication

———

To the human spirit that has lost touch with the reality of its spot of reason for existence.

To the person in existence that have lost their sense of purpose and the importance of their proximity to other lives around them.

To the individual experiencing a deep longing for joy and a natural need for fulfillment in life.

To the one silently battling to escape the rat race, to stop living a life of competition, and to stop allowing others dictate their life's course.

To you, the reader, I challenge you to re-capture your place of authority, place of influence, position of power, position of impact, and the significance of your reason for existence to humanity.

Acknowledgement

———

A tragedy would have unfolded, leading to the death of this book within me, were it not for the enduring impact of both living individuals and those who have passed but continue to shape my life from beyond their graveyards. Their unleashed potentials, too numerous to capture within the constraints of time, have played an important role in the creation of this book. I express heartfelt gratitude for channeling this book from within me with your inherent abilities and resources.

May your influence persist, transcending the boundaries of time, and may you endure until the moment when time interrupts eternity. Thank you sincerely.

Table Of Contents

————

Preface

———

The biggest hidden truth throughout history is that deep down, everyone on Earth is searching for a key simple solution to live an easier life; to hit it further, to live an effective life and welcome death anytime without any sense of regrets of the need to live back again. Many people wrongly believe that the answer must be complicated, but in reality, it is straightforward and easy to miss because it is not complex enough to grasp. As a result, we often overlook it. We need to be aware that our time on Earth is limited, so we should not abuse it holding onto these false assumptions. We must stop experimenting.

That is why I am much convinced without any doubt in my human spirit that, the greatest pandemic that plagues humanity is none other than emptiness itself. It appears that humanity has wandered away from the essence of meaning. Certain experts, boasting knowledge of the entire cosmos, awaken one day from their scholarly pursuits only to assert that life, in its grandeur, lacks any meaning. Initially, this notion seemed like an epiphany to humanity, a momentary solace in embracing the absence of reason of existence. Yet, this revelation ultimately led us into the quagmire of temporary folly, leaving us quietly desperate, trapped within ourselves, begrudgingly acknowledging our complete defeat.

Across the vast spectrum of human governance on Earth, none have managed to furnish us with the answers to unravel the mysterious journey so-called life. Some predecessors, choosing isolation from the world's clamor in pursuit of these answers, discovered themselves embroiled in an endless cycle of experimentation, concluding only that "life is too short—make every moment count." However, for most, this mantra seemed elusive, veiled in ambiguity.

Others emerged, proclaiming that "there is meaning to life," tantalizing us with the prospect of a universal answer. Regrettably, their assertions merely raised more questions than they answered, leaving humanity stranded in a sea of the fundamental human questions. Some, employing quotes that outsmarted our collective understanding, inadvertently plunged us into deeper depression than ever before.

They suggest that life's meaning hinges on the meaning one bestows upon it or how one chooses to live it. This, unfortunately, burdens humanity with the responsibility of crafting its own meaning. Consequently, humanity descended into a bottomless pit of self-negation, struggling to perceive any meaning and grappling with the futility of attempting to create one.

Efforts to generate meaning seemed futile and purposeless. Some advocated for self-investment, yet on this journey, the desire to improve, to thrive, remained absent. There was no joy, no end to the suffering wrought by this greatest pandemic of emptiness. Many felt powerless, realizing that external entities in the vast universe could not fill up this emptiness within themselves.

It appears we are trapped in a distorted view of life—wherein we oscillate between believing in existence and non-existence, attributing both meaning and meaninglessness to things. Despite this, we summon the motivation to awaken each day, engaging in activities we detest merely to live.

Individuals attempted various remedies—abstaining from vices, altering lifestyles, relationships, and environments—all in pursuit of liberation from the relentless grip of this global pandemic called emptiness. Yet, instead of respite, they found themselves confronted with an arduous quest to unearth a meaning, a reason to persist.

When confronted with the question of why they refrain from committing suicide, those suffering myriad torments—be it within prisons or any condition worst than hell—often cite slender threads anchoring them to life. Whether it is love for their children, a talent awaiting expression, or even lingering memories, the challenge lies in weaving these fragile strands into a coherent tapestry of meaning.

For some, the failure to uncover reason for existence ends in a tragic sacrifice—their lives laid bare upon the altar of death. Yet, this quest is not solely about enduring suffering and unfathomable horrors. Even amidst the chaos, some individuals find a raison d'être within their principles, morals, values, passions, convictions, or for the sake of someone for whom they are willing to sacrifice everything including their own lives.

Conversely, others inadvertently oscillate between attributing meaning and rendering everything meaningless. We legalize the termination of life in the womb, terming it "safe abortion," manufacture weapons that destroys us, and concoct substances that poison and destroy. We intoxicate our bodies with drugs, smother our lungs with smoke, and douse our livers with alcohol. Engulfed in illicit affairs, driven by the allure of wealth, we commodify our bodies, struggling relentlessly for survival and the elusive pursuit of happiness.

Such is the global pandemic that plagues us—a pandemic of emptiness, pervading every aspect of our existence.

So I have come to a humble conclusion that, the need for meaning is inherent in every human spirit. We all desire a meaning to our existence, a narrative that gives context to our lives beyond mere consumption of resources. It is a universal yearning to believe that our presence on Earth extends beyond the basic acts of survival. We seek meaning in the values we hold, our beliefs, educational achievements, and more. Whether it is through religion, meditation, scientific exploration, or the structures of our educational systems, we strive to find meaning in the apparent chaos of the universe. The burning question persists: Is there a meaning to this mysterious journey we call life?

Consider the scenario of dedicating decades to building a legacy, only to witness it crumble at the hands of those you raised. The emotional toll of investing time, energy, and hard-earned resources with your sweat and blood into nurturing your children, only to be met with ingratitude and resentment. Picture the heartbreak of giving a thoughtful gift, only to see it used callously, devoid of the sentimental value you attached to it. How does it feel when your passions and endeavors are dismissed as meaningless by those around you? These experiences, though deeply personal, resonate with a collective human greatest need for meaning.

Our yearning for meaning is not confined to personal achievements; it extends to the relationships we cultivate. The bonds we form with family, friends, and community hold profound significance in shaping our sense of purpose. The fragility of these connections, susceptible to misunderstandings, conflicts, and betrayals, adds another layer to our quest for meaning. How do we reconcile the need for meaning when our most cherished relationships falter or when the very essence of what we hold dear is questioned?

The pursuit of meaning is evident in the value we place on our contributions to society. The desire to make a difference, to leave a lasting impact, underscores our engagement in various fields. Whether through professional accomplishments, artistic endeavors, or acts of kindness, we seek validation for our existence in the positive influence we exert on the world around us. What happens when these efforts are met with indifference or criticism? How does one navigate the tension between personal fulfillment and societal expectations in the quest for meaning?

Our collective need for meaning extends beyond individual experiences and permeates societal structures. The institutions we create, be it religious, educational, or governmental, reflect our attempts to instill order and meaning into the fabric of our communities. The search for meaning becomes intertwined with cultural norms, moral frameworks, and shared beliefs that provide a collective narrative guiding our actions. Yet, even within these structures, conflicts arise, challenging the very foundations of our shared understanding of meaning.

Within the pages of this book, through patient exploration and contemplation, one could embark a journey of re-capturing the meaning of existence for their lives. This call transcend the constraints of religious or secular minds conviction and embrace the timeless knowledge, understanding and wisdom that lay within you.

CHAPTER

1

The Known Greatest Tragedy In Life

———

"The greatest pandemic that plagues humanity is none other than emptiness itself."

—*Paa Kwasi Mfoamfo*

The known greatest tragedy in life is life that fails to fulfill its reason for existence. That might not shock you because many of us, perhaps unwilling to admit it, try hard as we can to forget it, suffer from this affliction to the extent that we have lost touch with the reason of our existence. It is a grim reality that we, humanity live with a silent desperation, and some of us meet our end haunted by the vague feeling that we have missed the essence of reality.

As a collective, humanity grapples with a pervasive ignorance of reason for existence, permeating through nations, societies, communities, organizations, friendships, marriages, clubs, religions, tribes, and even down to individual creations. This ignorance of reason for existence breeds confusion, frustration, discouragement, and disillusionment. The world has transformed into a breeding ground for wars, massacres, hatred, stress, depression, hopelessness, and fear. Earth itself resembles a mother whose offspring, in this case, humanity, has lost the understanding of the rationale behind all aspects of life.

A historical perspective reveals that when humanity loses its sense of knowledge of reason for existence, the value of life diminishes, and the race to conform with the majority intensifies. A cursory glance at both past and present events paints a grim picture that demands our attention. Television screens daily broadcast a flood of distressing images—bloodshed, death, diplomacy, conflict, hatred, fear, poverty, starvation, rape, genocide, refugees, human migration, natural disasters, bombings, economic uncertainty, immigration, corporate corruption, moral decay, sexual revolution, and clashes of counter cultures.

Many of us often overlook the significance of being born and belonging to a nation. We may not fully grasp why our nation exists on a particular part of the Earth or appreciate the specifics of its geographical location—whether it faces constant scorching sun, enduring prolonged darkness, or situated on an island, desert, or by water bodies. Understanding the richness of our environment and the untapped resources within it, as well as considering our nation's proximity to others, is crucial. Recognizing how strategically divinity has place us in that specific location is vital.

Marriage, once a cornerstone of social development, now faces skepticism about its viability and validity. The soaring divorce rates contribute to the prevailing feelings of fear, hopelessness, disillusionment, and despair associated with marriage. Some opt for cohabitation without any formal commitment, creating a generation whose regard for the institution of marriage is rapidly eroding. Relationships are treated like commodities, tried on until they lose appeal, then discarded for the next fashionable option. We find ourselves in a disposable society, devoid knowledge of reason for existence.

Deep-seated ideologies crumble in the face of revolutionary changes. Sacred religious institutions morally decay under social pressures. Nations experience political re-engineering, frustration of traditional systems, social unrest, economic uncertainties, and institutionalized corruption. We construct buildings only to destroy them, develop weapons only to turn them against ourselves, invent healing medicines but withhold them from the sick, and enhance global communication through the internet only to destroy the moral principles and convictions of our children and their children's children.

In educational institutions, many pursue courses that lead to careers offering no fulfillment within their human spirit. Distracted by transient pleasures, some sacrifice their dignity and virginity, while others become pawns to political entities shaping their lives. This widespread loss knowledge of reason for existence permeates every facet of existence.

A whole generation, irrespective of nationality, seems disconnected from the values, morals, and convictions that build strong families, secure communities, healthy societies, and prosperous nations. Regardless of cultural, socioeconomic, or political circumstances, many endure lives characterized by daily drudgery. Even in affluent, industrialized states, where wealth and luxury abound, untold number of individuals grapple with depression, despair, anxiety, and emptiness. Possessions, fame, status, and power prove insufficient substitutes for a genuinely knowing one's reason for existence.

True liberation from this known greatest tragedy lies in re-capturing the reason for existence behind everything,

particularly our own existence, and committing to its
fulfillment.

THE WORLD OF DISILLUSIONMENT

The greatest pandemic that plagues humanity is none other
than emptiness itself. It appears that humanity has wandered
away from the essence of meaning. Certain experts, boasting
knowledge of the entire cosmos, awaken one day from their
scholarly pursuits only to assert that life, in its grandeur, lacks
any meaning. Initially, this notion seemed like an epiphany to
humanity, a momentary solace in embracing the absence of
reason of existence. Yet, this revelation ultimately led us into
the quagmire of temporary folly, leaving us quietly desperate,
trapped within ourselves, begrudgingly acknowledging our
complete defeat.

Across the vast spectrum of human governance on Earth, none
have managed to furnish us with the answers to unravel the
mysterious journey so-called life. Some predecessors, choosing
isolation from the world's clamor in pursuit of these answers,
discovered themselves embroiled in an endless cycle of
experimentation, concluding only that "life is too short—make
every moment count." However, for most, this mantra seemed
elusive, veiled in ambiguity.

Others emerged, proclaiming that "there is meaning to life,"
tantalizing us with the prospect of a universal answer.
Regrettably, their assertions merely raised more questions than
they answered, leaving humanity stranded in a sea of the
fundamental human questions. Some, employing quotes that

outsmarted our collective understanding, inadvertently plunged us into deeper depression than ever before.

They suggest that life's meaning hinges on the meaning one bestows upon it or how one chooses to live it. This, unfortunately, burdens humanity with the responsibility of crafting its own meaning. Consequently, humanity descended into a bottomless pit of self-negation, struggling to perceive any meaning and grappling with the futility of attempting to create one.

Efforts to generate meaning seemed futile and purposeless. Some advocated for self-investment, yet on this journey, the desire to improve, to thrive, remained absent. There was no joy, no end to the suffering wrought by this greatest pandemic of emptiness. Many felt powerless, realizing that external entities in the vast universe could not fill up this emptiness within themselves.

It appears we are trapped in a distorted view of life—wherein we oscillate between believing in existence and non-existence, attributing both meaning and meaninglessness to things. Despite this, we summon the motivation to awaken each day, engaging in activities we detest merely to live.

Individuals attempted various remedies—abstaining from vices, altering lifestyles, relationships, and environments—all in pursuit of liberation from the relentless grip of this global pandemic called emptiness. Yet, instead of respite, they found themselves confronted with an arduous quest to unearth a meaning, a reason to persist.

When confronted with the question of why they refrain from committing suicide, those suffering myriad torments—be it within prisons or any condition worst than hell—often cite slender threads anchoring them to life. Whether it is love for their children, a talent awaiting expression, or even lingering memories, the challenge lies in weaving these fragile strands into a coherent tapestry of meaning.

For some, the failure to uncover reason for existence ends in a tragic sacrifice—their lives laid bare upon the altar of death. Yet, this quest is not solely about enduring suffering and unfathomable horrors. Even amidst the chaos, some individuals find a raison d'être within their principles, morals, values, passions, convictions, or for the sake of someone for whom they are willing to sacrifice everything including their own lives.

Conversely, others inadvertently oscillate between attributing meaning and rendering everything meaningless. We legalize the termination of life in the womb, terming it "safe abortion," manufacture weapons that destroys us, and concoct substances that poison and destroy. We intoxicate our bodies with drugs, smother our lungs with smoke, and douse our livers with alcohol. Engulfed in illicit affairs, driven by the allure of wealth, we commodify our bodies, struggling relentlessly for survival and the elusive pursuit of happiness.

Such is the global pandemic that plagues us—a pandemic of emptiness, pervading every aspect of our existence. This emptiness pandemic is directly linked to our unmet human greatest needs. Our sense of emptiness arises from the existence of unfulfilled greatest needs, and it is important to address these greatest needs because ignoring them has led us to believe that life has no meaning, or that life's meaning is solely determined by our own perspectives, as the experts suggest. However, this emptiness is intricately connected to our reason for existing, causing some of us to silently feel convicted that there must be something that needs to be done, compelling us to exist in this particular period of history.

THE GREATEST NEEDS OF HUMANITY

The greatest needs of humanity are not shrouded in mystery but are observable in daily human actions and behaviors across the globe. If these needs remain concealed, it signals our high levels of ignorance about our own fundamental needs, essentially leading us to war against our very reason of existence. These greatest needs wield tremendous influence over the entire human race, driving every action and decision made on Earth. Whether rich, poor, or in-between, everyone grapples internally with unmet needs that leave their spirits empty.

These greatest needs transcend boundaries of race, culture, and creed, plaguing humanity universally and resulting in a pandemic of emptiness caused by their unfulfillment. They give rise to various industries, inspire art, literature, and shape entertainment. Moreover, they fuel the motivations behind corrupt leadership, self-destructive behaviors, and the struggles for power among political and religious figures.

From those living on the streets to those in positions of immense wealth and authority, everyone is driven by these needs. They prompt individuals into actions such as trading their bodies for sex, substance abuse, violence, and even tragic outcomes like suicides. Their influence extends to global crises like wars, economic instability, and the rapid emergence of new religious and social groups.

These greatest needs drive the most profound questions about our origins, purpose, identity, capabilities, and destinies. They underscore the very fabric of our existence and significantly determine our success or failure. Our lives pivot on these greatest needs; they are an inherent part of our human spirit and dictate the way we function. Satisfying our wants does not equate to fulfilling these greatest needs, as they exist on a deeper level, fundamental to our very being.

Failure to meet these greatest needs not only leads to personal malfunction but also inhibits individuals from comprehending and addressing the needs of others. These needs are the bedrock of existence, defining the reason for existence and quality of our lives. Human behavior is intricately tied to these needs, acting as sources of both fulfillment and emptiness. When unmet, they trigger a malfunction in our lives, affecting every individual on Earth.

Ultimately, these greatest needs of humanity form the central of our existence, steering our motivations, actions, and behaviors. Living a meaningful life on this planet hinges on effectively meeting these greatest needs. They hold the key to our fulfillment, and without their satisfaction, we, as humans, are prone to malfunction and dissatisfaction.

These greatest needs of humanity are the need for importance, meaning, power, success, and fulfilment. Let us explore into details each greatest needs of humanity as they are all tied to the reality of the reason for our existence, when overlooked it tends as the known greatest tragedy in life:

1. The Need for Importance: Every person on Earth has an innate desire to feel significant and valued. This desire is a crucial aspect of human existence, often unacknowledged but deeply felt. We all long to know that we matter, that we hold worth and are considered special. It is an essential need we are driven by, yet many deny its significance. Our pursuit of feeling valuable and respected drives us to great lengths, sometimes engaging in unusual behaviors. This quest for importance leads us to dress provocatively, alter our appearances in unconventional ways, or even adorn ourselves with extravagant items to stand out even with our sweat and blood from our lower incomes.

This quest is profound and touches upon our core need for recognition. Being ignored cuts deeply, causing emotional pain that most have experienced at some point. How does it feel when your heartfelt words are ignored or when someone dearest to you disregards you? The sting of being overlooked or dismissed affects us all. Being sidelined in a conversation, not receiving eye contact, or being excluded leaves a profound impact because we crave acknowledgment. Rejection, whether subtle or overt, triggers feelings of unworthiness and depression.

Feeling unimportant extends beyond personal interactions. It seeps into how our emotions are disregarded or our hardships go unnoticed. The absence of validation and reassurance leaves a void, making us silently question our importance. Even the fluctuation in social media attention can deeply affect our sense of importance, as we yearn for validation through subscribers, followers, likes, comments, and shares.

In its effect, the human greatest need for importance is a fundamental drive that influences our actions and emotions. It governs our pursuit of recognition and value, affecting us in various aspects of life, from personal interactions to our presence in the digital world.

2. The Need for Meaning: This greatest need for meaning is inherent in every human spirit. We all desire a meaning to our existence, a narrative that gives context to our lives beyond mere consumption of resources. It is a universal yearning to believe that our presence on Earth extends beyond the basic acts of survival. We seek meaning in the values we hold, our beliefs, educational achievements, and more. Whether it is through religion, meditation, scientific exploration, or the structures of our educational systems, we strive to find meaning in the apparent chaos of the universe. The burning question persists: Is there a meaning to this mysterious journey we call life?

Consider the scenario of dedicating decades to building a legacy, only to witness it crumble at the hands of those you raised. The emotional toll of investing time, energy, and hard-earned resources with your sweat and blood into nurturing your children, only to be met with ingratitude and resentment. Picture the heartbreak of giving a thoughtful gift, only to see it used callously, devoid of the sentimental value you attached to it. How does it feel when your passions and endeavors are dismissed as meaningless by those around you? These experiences, though deeply personal, resonate with a collective human greatest need for meaning.

Our yearning for meaning is not confined to personal achievements; it extends to the relationships we cultivate. The bonds we form with family, friends, and community hold profound significance in shaping our sense of purpose. The fragility of these connections, susceptible to misunderstandings, conflicts, and betrayals, adds another layer to our quest for meaning. How do we reconcile the need for meaning when our most cherished relationships falter or when the very essence of what we hold dear is questioned?

The pursuit of meaning is evident in the value we place on our contributions to society. The desire to make a difference, to leave a lasting impact, underscores our engagement in various fields. Whether through professional accomplishments, artistic endeavors, or acts of kindness, we seek validation for our existence in the positive influence we exert on the world around us. What happens when these efforts are met with indifference or criticism? How does one navigate the tension between personal fulfillment and societal expectations in the quest for meaning?

Our collective need for meaning extends beyond individual experiences and permeates societal structures. The institutions we create, be it religious, educational, or governmental, reflect our attempts to instill order and meaning into the fabric of our communities. The search for meaning becomes intertwined with cultural norms, moral frameworks, and shared beliefs that provide a collective narrative guiding our actions. Yet, even within these structures, conflicts arise, challenging the very foundations of our shared understanding of meaning.

3. The Need for Power: The craving for power is something we all have. It is about feeling like we are in charge or control of what happens to us. When life's circumstances take over, it hits us hard, leaving us feeling helpless and down. Imagine having loads of money, possessions, and everything you ever wanted, but then you get news that something deadly is lurking in your body. You instantly lose control over your health and your wealth becomes meaningless. Nothing is worst than the feeling to have everything in the world but not being able to enjoy it due to illness.

And when something happens to your loved ones, like your only child facing mental health issues or your marriage falling apart despite being known for your wisdom and riches, that feeling of powerlessness is crushing. Even in professional life, losing a job or facing a financial crisis can strip away that sense of control. When you can barely afford basic necessities due to an economic downturn, it is like losing power over your own life.

Imagine planning a life with someone, feeling so connected, only to be told they are leaving or found someone else. That sudden loss of a future you envisioned is devastating. And when someone you trusted betrays you, turning into an enemy or when you lose a loved one unexpectedly, it is like life is pulling the strings, and you have no say in it.

The greatest need for power drives people to extremes. Some fight and harm others, seeking positions or wealth, while others chase success in fields they are not passionate about. People strive to be around influential figures, sometimes resorting to manipulation and deceit to gain the position of power. Some focus on physical strength, others on spiritual practices, and some on acquiring knowledge, all in an attempt to gain control over circumstances.

In essence, this greatest need for power is deeply ingrained in us, driving us to go to great lengths to control our circumstances and lives.

4. The Need for Success: I still vividly remember the moment I realized that every human is on a pursuit for success, including myself. It was a shock! The desire to perceive oneself as successful is inherent in all of us. Failure is something we all detest, and that is why we strive to accomplish what we set out to achieve. It is one of the greatest human need. Falling short of our goals not only brings a sense of failure but also triggers profound inner conflict.

The lengths to which we go to attain success are remarkable. Each of us has our own definition of success. For some, it is acquiring material possessions like the latest phone, fashionable clothing, sneakers, or a stylish hairstyle. Others associate success with landing their dream job, getting married, excelling in exams, or gaining admission to a prestigious school. Some find success in promotions, being with a loved one, surpassing others, feeling superior, or being resourceful. It could also mean becoming the talk of the nation, witnessing their prayers answered, or experiencing new miracles. For some, success is synonymous with escaping tedious work and discovering the easiest ways to make money. There are those who measure success by being at the top of their class or even anticipating the failure of their peers.

The diverse manifestations of success are fueled by our innate and greatest need for it. We are driven by an internal desire to avoid failure and achieve a sense of accomplishment. When expectations fall short, the resultant inner conflict is deep. This greatest need for success is not merely a whimsical wish; it becomes an integral part of our motivation.

In this pursuit, we often find ourselves caught in the tension between societal expectations and our own definitions of success. The pressure to conform to conventional standards of success can be overwhelming, leading many to compromise their authentic desires. Yet, at the core of it all, the greatest need for success persists as a powerful driving force.

5. *The Need for Fulfilment:* The greatest human need for fulfillment is a powerful force that drives us in various ways.

Consider this: Why do well-off individuals in the wealthiest kingdom on Earth, who can barely spend a small fraction of their riches, resort to stealing? Why would someone who excels in academics, lands their dream job with a great salary, and owns everything they want, still submit their lives to suicide? Even couples married for decades split up and go their separate ways. Why do young, educated individuals distract themselves with drugs and alcohol? Why do people cheat on their partners whom they promised to stand by no matter what, even to go into the pit of hell with them? Why would a leader manipulate election figures and shut down internet networks to cling to position of power? Why is the porn website the most visited—as they say—despite public outcry against it? Why would a person lose their virginity early while another abstains? Why do some abruptly quit well-paying jobs to chase their dreams? Even those earning heaps of money from their filled of performances struggle to find happiness. Why would someone be in multiple relationships instead of just one? Why would the wealthiest person on Earth despite having everything necessary for a human to have to be human still feel sad? These questions point to a common theme—the greatest human need for fulfillment.

Humans inherently seek a sense of accomplishment and contentment. We strive to tick off achievements, whether it is owning possessions, completing tasks, or meeting societal expectations. However, despite attaining these goals, many of us grapple with a persistent emptiness. This emptiness manifests in various ways: substance abuse, infidelity, or even a reluctance to embrace one's true dreams despite financial stability.

The greatest human need for fulfillment is deeply ingrained in our psyche. It is the driving force behind our actions, compelling us to seek validation, reason, and a sense to be proud of ourselves. When unfulfilled, we experience an overwhelming emptiness that no material possessions or external accomplishments can fill. This sense of emptiness leads to suffering and a constant search for something more, something meaningful.

Remember, the greatest human need for fulfillment is a deeply personal journey. It is okay to feel disoriented or challenged along the way as you read the subsequent pages. Embracing this process can lead to a greater understanding of the meaning of existence for your life and pave the way towards your fulfillment.

Chapter 1: Principles To Think About Before You Take Your Last Breath

———

1. The known greatest tragedy in life is life that fails to fulfill its reason for existence.

2. The greatest pandemic that plagues humanity is none other than emptiness itself.

3. We all long to know that we matter, that we hold worth and are considered special. It is an essential need we are driven by, yet many deny its significance. Our pursuit of feeling valuable and respected drives us to great lengths, sometimes engaging in unusual behaviors. This quest for importance leads us to dress provocatively, alter our appearances in unconventional ways, or even adorn ourselves with extravagant items to stand out even with our sweat and blood from our lower incomes.

4. We all desire a meaning to our existence, a narrative that gives context to our lives beyond mere consumption of resources. It is a universal yearning to believe that our presence on Earth extends beyond the basic acts of survival. We seek meaning in the values we hold, our beliefs, educational achievements, and more. Whether it is through religion, meditation, scientific exploration, or the structures of our educational systems, we strive to find meaning in the

apparent chaos of the universe. The burning question persists: Is there a meaning to this mysterious journey we call life?

5. Nothing is worst than the feeling to have everything in the world but not being able to enjoy it due to illness.

6. The greatest need for power drives people to extremes. Some fight and harm others, seeking positions or wealth, while others chase success in fields they are not passionate about. People strive to be around influential figures, sometimes resorting to manipulation and deceit to gain the position of power. Some focus on physical strength, others on spiritual practices, and some on acquiring knowledge, all in an attempt to gain control over circumstances.

7. We are driven by an internal desire to avoid failure and achieve a sense of accomplishment. When expectations fall short, the resultant inner conflict is deep. This greatest need for success is not merely a whimsical wish; it becomes an integral part of our motivation.

8. The greatest human need for fulfillment is a powerful force that drives us in various ways. Consider this: Why do well-off individuals in the wealthiest kingdom on Earth, who can barely spend a small fraction of their riches, resort to stealing? Why would someone who excels in academics, lands their dream job with a great salary, and owns everything they want, still submit their lives to suicide? Even couples married for decades split up and go their separate

ways. Why do young, educated individuals distract themselves with drugs and alcohol? Why do people cheat on their partners whom they promised to stand by no matter what, even to go into the pit of hell with them? Why would a leader manipulate election figures and shut down internet networks to cling to position of power? Why is the porn website the most visited—as they say—despite public outcry against it? Why would a person lose their virginity early while another abstains? Why do some abruptly quit well-paying jobs to chase their dreams? Even those earning heaps of money from their filled of performances struggle to find happiness. Why would someone be in multiple relationships instead of just one? Why would the wealthiest person on Earth despite having everything necessary for a human to have to be human still feel sad? These questions point to a common theme—the greatest human need for fulfillment.

CHAPTER

2

The Unnamed Search In The Human Spirit

———

Humans naturally do not want to die because deep inside them, they know there are unfulfilled needs and an unending journey of an unnamed search within themselves. When a person has these greatest needs fulfilled and the search known and embodied within them, they welcome death without regrets.

The human unnamed search has persisted throughout history, often influenced by religious beliefs and scientific explanations. For countless years, humanity has grappled with the idea that life might lack meaning. This sentiment stems from two primary sources: the spiritual debt imposed by religion and the existential insights provided by scientific exploration.

Firstly, untold number of individuals silently feel burdened by the expectations set forth by their religious practices. Consider a scenario where an individual diligently performs ritualistic cleansings, engages in devout worship, and commits to daily prayers, yet finds a persistent sense of emptiness. The spiritual obligations, though rigorously observed, fail to satiate a deeper longing for meaning. Similarly, prolonged meditation or prayer marathons might lead to a realization that, despite these efforts, life's essence remains elusive, prompting a void within.

Secondly, scientific perspectives often contribute to the crisis of meaning. Some assert that life, originating from a random interplay of elements and biological processes, inherently lacks meaning. From a scientific standpoint, life's meaning might be perceived as bleak, relentless, and narrow—a survival-driven impulse shared with all living entities, from single-celled organisms to complex beings like humans. This understanding, while seemingly rational, undermines the existence of an objective meaning.

Moreover, the fluidity of meanings in society adds to the confusion. Concepts of gender identity, for instance, constantly evolve, challenging established norms and altering our perceptions of fundamental aspects of life. This societal flux further accentuates the quest for meaning, leaving individuals grappling with their identity and meaning for their existence.

Our individual experiences also contribute significantly to the perception of life's meaninglessness. Relationships losing their initial intensity, repeated heartbreaks. Conversations lose their depth, vulnerable feelings remain unshared, and a sense of hollowness pervades.

Similarly, the pursuit of knowledge in academic realms can be marred by a sense of disconnection. Enrolling in courses, hoping to unravel personal confusion, often leads to disappointment when the topics appear dull and unrelated to one's existential quandaries. The pursuit of education feels devoid of meaning.

Even in the professional sphere, lucrative jobs fail to offer the profound satisfaction sought by many of us. Despite earning decent wages, we may grapple with the insignificance of our contributions. The job, seemingly detached from our core identity, raises questions about the necessity of our human involvement when artificial intelligence could seemingly perform the tasks just as efficiently.

This cumulative weight of spiritual, scientific, societal, and personal factors leads to an unnamed searching within the human spirit—a persistent belief that something beyond the mundane exists. This unnamed search represents a collective longing for a deeper, more profound meaning in life, one that transcends the limitations imposed by religion, scientific explanations, societal constructs, and personal experiences.

This search is not merely a quest for an answer but an ongoing journey—a testament to humanity's intrinsic desire to find purpose in a universe that often appears indifferent. It reflects an innate curiosity, a yearning for a more profound understanding of existence that lies beyond the surface.

THE WAKING UP ALARM THAT EXPOSES HUMANITY'S EMPTINESS

Humans naturally do not want to die because deep inside them, they know there are unfulfilled needs and an unending journey of an unnamed search within themselves. When a person has these greatest needs fulfilled and the search known and embodied within them, they welcome death without regrets.

For untold years, scientists became open to the universe and claimed someone must have orchestrated it. They try to explain that there must be a higher force behind the universe because of its precision. Planets not only revolve in specific orbits around stars but also avoid crashing into each other. They suggest that someone may have set this motion, indicating a potential meaning behind it all.

They studied the universe, formulated laws to explain it, and even re-discovered that insects are attracted to specific plants, certain animals leave certain places to survive, while others thrive in those same places. They even explored using our kitchen waste and excreta for beneficial meanings, finding ways to regenerate or generate energy.

Religious minds silently grapple among themselves, questioning the significance beyond worship, prayer, and rituals. Some assert that after performing their activities, they wonder what more there is on Earth. Others, inspired by historical great thinkers through meditation and philosophical embodiment, sense a deeper meaning.

Some, after achieving academic success, realize they are trapped in a slave machinery called job due to economic crises, doing what they are not passionate about and for but they have to do it inorder to survive. Some find marriage lacking despite having attention, care, love, children, wealth, and properties. Those enlightened in various ways strive to answer life's questions, impressing us with powerful words, yet challenged by the "why?" of life.

It is not a shocking revelation that every human knows where they are and how they got there, by various means of transportation or something. But the question that concerns us most is "why am I here?" This question delves deep! Because the greatest question in life is "why," offering fulfillment to the "what?" of life.

For untold years, the wealthiest and wisest person who ever live, King Solomon wrote a book full of sarcasm, serving as a commentary on humanity's emptiness. It teases humanity, exposes their accomplishments as meaningless, presenting positives as negatives and vice versa as stated in *Ecclesiastes 1:2-11 & 14; 2:1-11,17-23; 3:22; 4:7-8; 5:8-17; 6:7-12; 8:7-8,16-17; 9:3-6; 11:5,7-10; 12:1-8* of the Bible to which I have decoded what he said into these words, as it unfolds:

In this transient world where days pass swiftly,

Everything appears as a fleeting haze.

The Teacher, with bitter wit, declares,

"Meaningless! Oh, meaninglessness, in every aspect!"

Human toil under the scorching sun,

What reward is there when all is said and done?

Generations come and go,

Yet the earth endures, an eternal cycle.

The sun rises and sets,

A constant cycle without remorse.

The wind blows from south to north,

An endless journey back and forth.

Streams flow into the sea,

Yet the sea never refuses.

All things become tiresome,

The eyes and ears constantly seek novelty.

What has been done will be done again,

Nothing is truly new under the sun.

Is there anything genuinely fresh and vibrant?

No, it existed long before our time.

There's no recollection of past generations,

Their stories remain untold.

All actions under the sun,

Are merely a pursuit of fleeting dreams.

"I'll seek pleasure," I said, jokingly,

But even that left me feeling distressed.

Laughter, pleasure, all prove to be in vain,

Merely fleeting and passing moments.

I indulged in wine and folly,

Yet I still followed the path of wisdom.

I built, planted, amassed great wealth,

But found no solace in this world's obscurity.

I denied myself nothing, pursued every desire,

Yet found no satisfaction, life felt grim.

All my toil, all my struggles,

Ended up amounting to nothing, a futile existence.

So I despised life under the harsh glare of the sun,

Everything felt meaningless, beyond repair.

Who knows what the future holds?

Despite all our efforts, treasures, and wealth.

Man labours tirelessly day and night,

Yet what is the gain in the fading light?

All days filled with pain and sorrow,

No rest, no joy, no hope for the morrow.

So enjoy your work, enjoy your circumstances,

For who knows what fate time will bring?

Yet amidst all this vanity, I've witnessed,

The oppression of the poor, justice remains unseen.

The pursuit of wealth is an endless race,

Bringing no peace, no lasting grace.

The more we have, the more we desire,

Yet ultimately, we find ourselves in the grave.

In life's fleeting shadow, we traverse,

What is the purpose, what is the signal?

No one knows what the future holds,

No one controls, the future unfolds.

So enjoy the light, relish the warmth of the sun,

For darkness is inevitable, we know.

Remember your Creator in your youth,

Before age obscures your truth.

Before the days of trouble arrive,

And life's joys become numb.

Remember before the silver cord is cut,

Before all is lost, and life is attempted.

"Meaningless! Meaningless!" cries the Teacher,

In this world of fleeting highs.

Everything, absolutely everything, he proclaims,

Is merely a pursuit of dreams.

Let us take a moment to admire King Solomon. He possessed everything many of us are striving for today. He aimed to spare us from the haunting feeling of emptiness. He expressed that pursuing material things leads to a hollow end. Some of us are already caught in this emptiness. What is he trying to convey to humanity? King Solomon is highlighting the emptiness of chasing after top grades in school, seeking a high-paying job, gathering immense wealth, fame, and accolades. He ponder whether it is tragic to be renowned, beautiful, handsome, wise, or foolish, yet feel unfulfilled despite achieving all what you set your eyes on to attain.

Imagine being celebrated globally, having unparalleled success, being technologically ahead, or being perceived as the most powerful or righteous individual globally. Envision marrying someone with extraordinary love, possessing vast industries and billions in the bank, along with all the luxuries of modern life. Yet, despite having it all, the satisfaction remains elusive. Deep inside, there is a silent, desperate frustration.

This sense of emptiness and silent frustration stems from not comprehending one's unique meaning of existence for their life—a plan set by God who lives outside time and cannot be proven by humanity's senses, theory, deep philosophical words, or technology, placed humanity in time on Earth. All these accomplishments and possessions are tools for fulfilling a predetermined meaning of existence before our time ends on

Earth. Failure to grasp our individual's meaning of existence for our lives leads to a lifelong frustration, haunting us to our graveyard.

King Solomon stresses that knowing the 'why' of existence outweighs knowing the 'what'. Understanding one's meaning of existence is crucial, as it dictates the fulfillment of one's life. Without this understanding, even the most extraordinary achievements or possessions would not fill the void within.

WHAT IS THE NAME OF YOUR SEARCH FOR THE MEANING OF EXISTENCE FOR YOUR LIFE

Many collective names are given to the meaning of existence in our lives on planet Earth. Some refer to it as a "calling," "anointing," "prophecy," "will of God," "chosen," "appointed," or "ordained," from a religious perspective. Others prefer to use words like "assignment," "role," "duty," "function," "authority," "career," "work," "leadership," "course," or "life's path" to describe this meaning. We even construct philosophies, establish institutions, create organizations, and develop doctrines and theories around it.

Some who refer to it as a "calling," believe that we have been summoned by divinity at a specific point in history. Others speak of an "anointing," suggesting certain individuals are marked in unique areas of life. Some seeing it as a "prophecy," declaring our presence on Earth for a specific time from prophetic standpoint. "Will of God" signifies a divine intention on Earth, reliant on humanity's involvement, thus also by some.

There are those who prefer "chosen," suggesting uniqueness among the called, and "appointed," viewing our existence as a divine decision beyond parental planning. 'Ordained' highlights a destined something to serve the world, while "assignment" implies a specific task meant for us alone to do and complete.

For some, it is a "role" or "duty," emphasizing our essential function in the universe. "Function" and "authority" stress our integral part and sanctioned domain. "Career" signifies an inner calling, while "work" emphasizes doing something more fulfilling beyond mere existence. "Leadership" denotes leading oneself, not blindly following others (or any concept of leadership you may know).

To others, it is a "course" leading to success, while those attuned to the universe see it as "life's path," a destined journey to experience and live out. What name do you prefer to describe the meaning of existence for humanity's lives?

Our deep motivation to understand the meaning of our existence leads us to assign all these names to it. To avoid complicating things for modern minds, I prefer to use the word "purpose" frequently throughout this book to facilitate a deeper and easier understanding of the meaning of our existence on planet Earth. We will explore this concept in more detail in the following pages.

Chapter 3: Principles To Think About Before You Take Your Last Breath

———

1. Cumulative weight of spiritual, scientific, societal, and personal factors leads to an unnamed searching within the human spirit—a persistent belief that something beyond the mundane exists. This unnamed search represents a collective longing for a deeper, more profound meaning in life, one that transcends the limitations imposed by religion, scientific explanations, societal constructs, and personal experiences. This search is not merely a quest for an answer but an ongoing journey—a testament to humanity's intrinsic desire to find purpose in a universe that often appears indifferent. It reflects an innate curiosity, a yearning for a more profound understanding of existence that lies beyond the surface.

2. Humans naturally do not want to die because deep inside them, they know there are unfulfilled needs and an unending journey of an unnamed search within themselves. When a person has these greatest needs fulfilled and the search known and embodied within them, they welcome death without regrets.

3. It is not a shocking revelation that every human knows where they are and how they got there, by

various means of transportation or something. But the question that concerns us most is "why am I here?" This question delves deep! Because the greatest question in life is "why," offering fulfillment to the "what?" of life.

CHAPTER

3

In Pursuit Of The Meaning Of Existence

For Your Life

———

T he deepest yearning of the human spirit is to attain a sense of ultimate fulfillment. The pursuit of this ultimate fulfillment in life stands as humanity's paramount pursuit. Not a single soul on Earth desires to endure unending suffering, frustration, anxiety, depression, or inner trauma. We all strive to discover this profound sense of contentment within ourselves. Consider this: as social beings, our most fulfilling moments often arise from connections, such as revealing our intimate physical and psychological selves to a partner, forming friendships where substantial aspects of our lives are shared, or embarking on a journey to a new country, overcoming linguistic and cultural barriers through engaging conversations with strangers. Furthermore, there is distinct sense of fulfillment derived from resolving confusion and puzzlement about ourselves or the world.

It is important to realize that your life's fulfillment hinges upon recapturing the meaning of existence for your life—termed "purpose"—and ardently pursuing it with unwavering commitment. Anything less would render life an adversary and death a companion. We have erroneously intertwined accomplishment with satisfaction and success with fulfillment. Many individuals have achieved remarkable feats and even secured a place in the Guinness World Records, yet they remain unsatisfied. Conversely, there are those who bask in substantial success but lack fulfillment. Success lies in fulfilling one's purpose, adhering to its dictates. Therefore, success can solely be defined by purpose and gauged by one's commitment to it. Fulfillment only materializes when purpose is re-captured and lived out. Hence, it is imperative for us to delve into the foundational principles of purpose and deduce the definition of purpose to avoid losing touch with reality.

THE FOUNDATIONAL PRINCIPLES OF PURPOSE

1. Purpose precedes creation.

Before any manufacturer creates a product, they first determine its purpose. Thus, the prerequisite for creating something is its purpose. Purpose represents the original idea behind creating something, existing in the mind of its creator. It essentially embodies the "why" in the creator's mind. This principle is fundamental in the manufacturing world, never skipped by any manufacturer. No manufacturer creates a product and then decides to discover its purpose through experimentation afterward. Essentially, before a product materializes, its purpose already exists in the creator's mind as an idea.

Therefore, every product starts as an idea within the creator's mind before becoming a tangible product. That clearly shows that, everything in existence has a creator and a purpose. Meeting the creator of something before its creation would mean encountering the essence of that creation within them. For instance, meeting Albert Einstein at 14 would have meant encountering the theory of relativity that he later developed at 26. Similarly, shaking hands with Alexander Graham Bell before age 29 would have been shaking hands with the concept of the telephone inside him, same thing applies to meeting Steve Jobs, the co-inventor of Apple Macintosh computer.

Ideas hold immense power and significance, shaping reality. They can solve problems but can also create destructive outcomes, such as terrorism or racism when distorted. Therefore, a thing's purpose exists solely in its creator's mind.

Purpose precedes creation, residing solely in the mind of the creator. Finding the purpose of a thing involves seeking it from the creator of the thing.

2. Purpose is built into creation.

Purpose is not an afterthought or an external layer added to things. Instead, it stands as an integral and inherent aspect of what a thing is. It is the natural makeup, the DNA, if you will, of every entity in existence. Purpose is not a skill acquired or a trait learned; it is innate, existing from the very moment of creation.

Consider purpose as the unseen blueprint, outlining the qualities and characteristics that define a thing from its inception. These qualities are not acquired through external influences but are part of the thing's essence, shaping its identity from the beginning. Purpose, therefore, cannot be discovered in the conventional sense; it can only be re-discovered. It is not a puzzle waiting to be solved but a fundamental aspect waiting to be acknowledged.

This principle is not limited to inanimate objects or the natural world; it extends to us—humanity. The purposes of our lives are not something we create; instead, we have the opportunity to re-capture them. Like a hidden treasure waiting to be unearthed, purpose comes with the product, inherent in our existence, not external to it.

In the quest to understand the purpose built into creation, it becomes evident that purpose is not a latecomer to the scene; it is a foundational element. Just as a tree bears fruits according to its kind, so does purpose manifest in alignment with the essence of the created thing. It is not a transient companion that can be abandoned at will; it is an inseparable companion woven into the very fabric of existence.

That is why we often find ourselves driven by an inner force, an unspoken knowing that we were purposed for something. It is a sensation deep within our human spirits, an intrinsic understanding that goes beyond mere cognition. This feeling is not something dictated by external voices; no one explicitly told us there is purpose for our lives, we feel it resonating within us.

3. Purpose determines function.

The purpose of a thing determines what it does or how it works, thus called function. Function is what something does or how it operates. It is directly linked to the purpose. For instance, the function of a knife is to slice through objects, the function of a chair is to support someone sitting, and the function of a smartphone is to make calls, send messages, and more.

Think of a car. Its purpose is transportation, and its functions are to move people from one place to another efficiently and safely. Now, the car's functions—like having wheels, an engine, seats, and a steering wheel—are all designed to serve this transportation purpose. If any of these components does not contribute to this purpose, it might not be included in the design.

Take smartphones. Their purpose is communication and access to information. Hence, their functions include calling, messaging, internet browsing, and various apps—all serving this purpose.

In living organisms, every part has a purpose that determines its function. For instance, the heart's purpose is to pump blood, and its function is to contract rhythmically to facilitate circulation.

In essence, "purpose determines function" is a fundamental concept across various aspects of life. Understanding why something exists or was created helps us comprehend what is supposed to do it and how it is supposed to operate or work.

4. Purpose dictates design.

The purpose of something determines how it is created or structured. This principle applies across various domains, from architecture to transportation, and even in everyday objects.

Thus, purpose becomes the guiding factor that shapes the entire design process.

For instance, think about a chair. Its purpose is to provide support and comfort for a person to sit. This purpose dictates its design – it needs a stable structure, a seat at a certain height, and a backrest for support. If the chair's purpose was different, say, for artistic expression rather than sitting, its design would significantly differ.

In architecture, the purpose of a building influences its design profoundly. A hospital requires specific layouts for patient care, while a shopping mall focuses on maximizing retail space and customer flow. The purpose dictates the architectural elements, such as room allocation, entryways, and infrastructure.

The purpose of a vehicle determines its design – a family car focuses on safety and space, while a sports car emphasizes speed and performance. This principle extends from the overall structure to the specifics of engines, seats, and even materials used.

Purpose plays a significant role in a product aesthetic appeal. The design elements, such as color, shape, and texture, are chosen to align with the intended purpose. For instance, a product designed for children may feature vibrant colors and playful shapes to engage their imagination and capture their attention. Understanding the purpose behind a creation can enhance our appreciation for its design. By recognizing the thought and intention that went into shaping an object, we can gain a deeper understanding of its value and significance.

5. *Purpose protects creation.*

Purpose is like a guiding force that shapes the perfect setting for something to function at its best. Take a fish, for instance – its purpose is to swim, and this purpose safeguards it from attempting to live outside of water. Similarly, a bird would not plunge into water because its purpose directs it away from such actions. Understanding the purpose of an electric iron prevents it from submerging it into water by an individual. In the same vein, comprehending your purpose acts as a shield, helping you navigate your surroundings wisely.

When we talk about purpose protecting creation, it is about finding the optimal conditions for things to thrive. Just as a fish flourishes in water, each entity has its purpose, and recognizing that purpose is crucial for its protection. This recognition acts as a compass, guiding the entity away from environments or situations that could be detrimental.

Knowing your purpose serves as a filter for decision-making. It helps you discern where to be, the kind of people to surround yourself with, and the paths to tread or avoid. It acts as a protective barrier, steering you away from actions that might jeopardize your well-being or hinder your growth.

Consider a fish out of water – it is out of its purposeful environment, struggling and vulnerable. Similarly, when individuals are unaware of their purpose, they may find themselves in situations that are not conducive to their growth or well-being. Purpose becomes a shield, safeguarding us from wandering into places or relationships that may not align with our intended path.

Purpose also plays a role in creating boundaries. Just as a bird would not explore underwater realms due to its purpose of flying, understanding your purpose helps establish limits. It empowers you to say no to situations or opportunities that do not align with your overarching goals. In this way, purpose acts as a guardian, protecting your energy and resources for endeavors that truly matter.

Understanding and embracing your purpose is akin to donning armor, shielding you from the pitfalls of aimless wandering and empowering you to navigate life with intention and resilience.

6. Purpose determines potential.

The purpose of a thing determines its inherent capabilities. This implies that the design and function of a thing play a crucial role in defining its effectiveness and possibilities.

Consider a simple tool, like a hammer. Its purpose is to drive nails into surfaces. The potential of the hammer is intricately tied to this specific function. It possesses a sturdy handle and a heavy head precisely crafted for pounding nails effortlessly. If one were to attempt using the hammer for a purpose outside its design, say, as a cooking utensil, the potential is untapped, and the tool becomes less effective.

This principle extends beyond tangible objects into the realm of human endeavors. Take education, for instance. The purpose of education is multifaceted, aiming to impart knowledge, foster critical thinking, and prepare individuals for various aspects of life. The potential of an educational system is intricately linked to its ability to fulfill these purposes. A well-structured and comprehensive education system equips individuals with the skills and knowledge needed to navigate and contribute to society effectively.

In the professional sphere, the purpose of a job position determines the potential impact an employee can have. If someone is hired for a specific role, their potential is maximized when they align their skills and efforts with the objectives of that role. For instance, a sales representative's potential is best realized when they excel at connecting with clients and closing deals, as this aligns with the purpose of their position.

This principle also resonates in the realm of technology. Take smartphones as an example. The purpose of a smartphone is not limited to making calls; it encompasses various functions like internet browsing, photography, and productivity tools. The potential of a smartphone is fully realized when users leverage its diverse features to meet their individual needs. If someone only uses a smartphone for calls and neglects its other capabilities, they are not tapping into its full potential.

In a broader societal context, the purpose of institutions shapes their potential impact. Governments, for instance, exist to provide governance, security, and public services. The potential effectiveness of a government is contingent on its ability to fulfill these roles and address the needs of its citizens. If a government strays from its fundamental purposes, its potential to positively impact society diminishes.

In essence, purpose serves as a guiding principle for optimizing outcomes and realizing the untapped ability trapped in various aspects of life.

7. Purpose measures success.

A clear purpose in one's endeavors is a key determinant of success. In essence, the pursuit of a well-defined purpose provides direction, motivation, and a yardstick for evaluating achievements.

Purpose involves aligning one's personal values, passions, and aspirations with their actions. Purpose serves as a compass, guiding individuals and organizations towards meaningful goals. When there is a strong sense of purpose, it becomes a powerful motivator, fueling perseverance in the face of challenges. Success is not solely measured by external metrics like wealth or recognition but also by the fulfillment derived from pursuing a purposeful path.

Success, when measured through the lens of purpose, is not just about reaching a destination but also about the journey itself. It involves progress and growth aligned with one's purpose. For example, a person aiming to improve the well-being of others might measure success by the positive impact they make in people's lives rather than just financial gains.

A clear purpose provides focus, helping individuals and organizations prioritize their efforts. This clarity reduces distractions and enables more effective decision-making. Success, then, is not scattered or arbitrary; it is the result of intentional actions guided by a well-defined purpose.

When purpose is deeply embedded in one's pursuits, it generates intrinsic motivation. Unlike extrinsic factors such as external rewards or societal expectations, intrinsic motivation arises from within. Succes is characterized by a genuine passion for what one does, contributing to a more sustainable and fulfilling sense of achievement.

The pursuit of purpose is closely linked to personal and collective well-being. Success intertwined with purpose, contributes to a sense of fulfillment and satisfaction. Success goes beyond material achievements, encompassing mental, emotional, and social well-being.

8. Purpose provides vision.

Purpose is a fundamental cornerstone in understanding how our aspirations and direction in life are intertwined. It serves as our guiding light, shaping our actions and decisions. It is the North Star that guides our journey through life. When we talk about vision, we are referring to the mental image or conceptual view of where we want to be in the future. It is like a roadmap guiding us towards our goals.

Think of purpose as the seed from which vision grows. Without a purpose, it becomes challenging to envisage where we want to go or what we want to achieve. Just as a plant needs a seed to sprout and grow, our aspirations and ambitions need a purpose to take root and flourish.

For instance, consider an individual passionate about environmental conservation. Their purpose might be to safeguard the planet for future generations. This purpose then shapes their vision, envisioning a world with clean energy, reduced pollution, and thriving ecosystems. This vision motivates them to take action, whether through advocating for policy changes, adopting sustainable practices, or raising awareness.

Our purpose acts as a lens through which we view our future. It provides clarity and direction, helping us prioritize our goals and make decisions aligned with our values. Without a clear purpose, our vision might be blurry or undefined, making it challenging to work towards specific objectives.

Moreover, purpose has a profound impact on motivation. When we have a strong sense of purpose, it fuels our passion and commitment. It becomes the driving force behind our actions, even during challenging times. Imagine a business with a purpose to provide access to education for underprivileged children. This purpose inspires their vision of a world where every child has equal opportunities. It motivates them to innovate, create partnerships, and overcome obstacles to fulfill their mission.

In effect, purpose serves as the foundation upon which our vision is built. It shapes our aspirations, guides our actions, and gives meaning to our lives. By understanding and nurturing our purpose, we can cultivate a clear and inspiring vision for our future, empowering us to strive towards our goals with purposeful intent.

9. Purpose maintains objectivity.

Purpose provides a clear and specific use for everything, steering away from subjective feelings or personal inclinations. It acts as a guiding principle that helps individuals utilize things for their intended use, thereby preventing the distortion or misuse of those items based on personal emotions.

When we consider purpose in relation to objectivity, it is important to grasp that purpose is intrinsically tied to specificity. Each item or action has a designated purpose that delineates its intended function. This purpose serves as a blueprint, guiding us on how to use or interact with that specific thing. For instance, a hammer is purposefully designed to drive nails into surfaces. Using it for a different purpose, such as a paperweight, may negate its primary objective and efficiency.

Purpose also helps in avoiding relativism. Relativism occurs when the understanding or usage of something becomes relative to individual perspectives or situational needs. By adhering to the designated purpose of an object or action, we maintain an objective standard, ensuring that the item serves its intended function consistently across various contexts.

Furthermore, purpose safeguards the identity of things. Objects have inherent characteristics that define them and give them meaning. When utilized according to their purpose, they retain their essence and uniqueness. However, deviating from their intended purpose can lead to a loss of identity, transforming them into something different altogether.

Consider a knife, for instance. Its purpose is to cut various materials efficiently. If used for a different purpose, say as a screwdriver, the knife's identity and effectiveness in cutting might be compromised. It might even risk damage or injury due to improper use, highlighting the significance of adhering to its intended purpose.

Emotions and personal feelings can sometimes cloud judgment, leading individuals to generate new purpose or misuse objects based on how they feel at a given moment. However, understanding and adhering to an object's purpose counteracts this tendency, ensuring a more rational and objective approach to its usage.

Ultimately, purpose maintains objectivity by anchoring us to the intended function of things, steering us away from subjective interpretations or arbitrary applications. It upholds the integrity of objects, ensuring they remain true to their essence and function. This adherence to purpose fosters clarity, reliability, and efficiency in our interactions with ourselves and the world around us.

10. Purpose measures life.

The essence of measuring life's value lies not in the duration it exists, but rather in the fulfillment of its intended purpose. Think of it this way: the significance of a life is not solely determined by how long it lasts, but by the impact it makes through achieving its intended goals.

Consider a clock. Its life is not about how many years it ticks away, but rather in its primary purpose of telling time accurately. If it fulfills this function effectively, its life is considered purposeful and valuable.

Similarly, for humans, the essence of existence is not solely about the number of years lived, but the contribution made towards their intended purposes. Every individual has unique aspirations, dreams, and roles to play in society. A person's life gains depth and significance when they actively work towards fulfilling these purposes.

Measuring life's worth through its purpose is very important. It emphasizes the inherent value of goals, intentions, and actions rather than simply the passage of time. It encourages individuals to reflect on their objectives and how they contribute to the world around them.

Purpose gives direction and meaning to life. It is like a guiding compass that helps individuals navigate the journey, making choices and decisions that align with their intended objectives. Without purpose, life can feel aimless, lacking in fulfillment and significance.

Imagine someone passionate about environmental conservation. Their life's purpose might revolve around protecting and preserving nature. Now, regardless of the number of years they live, the value of their life is measured by the extent to which they contribute to this cause. Whether it is planting trees, advocating for policies, or educating others about sustainability, their impact determines the richness and value of their life.

Ultimately, the measure of a life well-lived lies in the alignment of actions, choices, and efforts with one's purpose. It is about making the most of the time one has by investing it in endeavors that resonate with their deepest aspirations, values, and convictions. In doing so, individuals create a legacy that extends beyond their years, graveyard and continues to impact the world. In effect, the true measure of life is not the number of years lived, but the extent to which one lives with purpose, contributing meaningfully to the world around them.

DEFINING THE MEANING OF EXISTENCE FOR YOUR LIFE—PURPOSE

To define the meaning of our lives, which is also known as purpose, we will examine different definitions. This will help us understand what it means for our lives to have a purpose before delving deeper into the heart purpose for our lives in the following chapters. Now, let us explore the different definitions of the purpose of our lives that I have summarized below:

- **Purpose is the original idea for the creation of a thing that was in the mind of the creator of a thing.**

Everything has a creator and the purpose for which the creator created it. The purpose of a thing is only found in the mind of its creator, not within the thing itself. Effectively, if you want to understand how a thing was meant to function, never ask the thing itself, but rather its creator. If you want to comprehend how a car functions, you do not ask the car; you ask the car's creator. Similarly, if you seek to understand how your smartphone operates, you do not ask the smartphone because it is not smart enough to figure out its purpose; you ask the creator of the smartphone. If you cannot find the creator, they often provide a small booklet called a manual, which encapsulates the original idea for the creation of the thing. Alternatively, they attach their original idea to the packaging of the thing, be it a wrapper, box, or container, indicating a section boldly labelled as "usage," "directions," "function." Or add their image—thus logo or name, so that you can come to them directly to get their original idea on "why" of their created thing. Or better still, some direct you to an authorized person sanctioned and endowed with the original idea by them to re-veal to you the purpose of their creation.

If everything has a purpose, then there is a purpose for life, which suggests there is a creator of life. The creator of life is not a mystery to be explored and figured out; the Creator of life is God. He created a life called humanity, which includes your life. Since there is a creator for your life, it follows that there is a purpose for your life. God, who created our lives, did not leave us in mystery to wonder and experiment with our lives to discern our purpose. He imprinted His image on us, His created beings, as stated in Genesis 1:26, *"Then God said: 'Let Us make man in our image...'"* This means that only God, the Creator of your life, knows the original idea for our creation. Anyone apart from God is merely guessing, experimenting, presuming, or assuming our purpose, and despite their sincere attempts—whether psychologically, philosophically, biologically, or theologically—they can be faithfully wrong if not authorized with God's original idea for our lives. That is why nothing is worst than being sincere about something and be faithfully wrong. Because being sincere does not mean you are right, you can be faithfully wrong about that thing.

The only authorized person, whom the Creator of our lives has sanctioned and endowed with His original idea for our existence on this planet Earth, is Jesus Christ. He was first introduced as the "Word," signifying the "idea carrier," as stated in John 1:1-4:

> *"In the beginning was the Word, and the Word was with God, and the Word was God. He was with God in the beginning. Through Him all things were made; without Him nothing was made that has been made. In Him was life, and that life was the light (pure knowledge; truth) of men."*

Jesus Christ is God's original idea on two legs, thus in human form. Therefore, you should turn to Jesus Christ not to embrace a religion or confine yourself to narrow church meetings, but to re-discover the life you were born to live. Hence, one of His famous statements is, *"I am the Way, the Truth, and the Life. No one comes to the Father (God) except through Me" (John 14:6).* In other words, Jesus Christ asserts that He is the only authorized person (the Way) who knows God's original idea (the Truth) about your existence (the Life). And if you still doubt that He is the only one who knows the purpose for your life, Jesus Christ reveals that God, the Creator of your life, has made Him the only person who can guide you to reach Him, *"...No one comes to the Father (God) except through Me."* That is deep!

- **Purpose is the primary cause for the existence of something.**

This contradicts what the experts say: purpose is not something you find but something you create. In other words, they assert that purpose is relative; there is no objectivity in everything. It is the meaning you give it, not the meaning built into it. Purpose is inherent in creation because it is built into creation, not what you try to make it be. Therefore, you cannot monetary, intellectually, awakeningly, or spiritually create your own purpose for life.

It is surprising that many do not know the purpose of a knife, we use it to stab and kill ourselves. We misunderstand the purpose of a marital relationship. Our lack of understanding of use of substances like marijuana, cocaine, cigarettes, and alcohol leads to the abuse of it. Similarly, many misunderstand the purpose of their rectums, trying to make them entrances instead of exits. This ignorance results in self-violation and frustration when you overlook or change the purpose of something.

Look at the primary cause of humanity's creation in Genesis 1:26: *"Then God said: 'Let Us make man in Our image, according to Our likeness; let them have dominion... over all the earth."* Dominion means sovereignty, administration, management, rulership, leadership, influence, and authority. If drugs or fleeting pleasures dominate you, you are in trouble. If money influences every decision, you are dominated by money. If a spouse rules over you, it is a misunderstanding of marriage's purpose.

The purpose of humanity is not created by humans, it is re-discovered to live it by humans. If what you are doing dominates you, it is a sign that it is not your destined path on Earth. You were inherently designed for rulership, leadership, influence, impact, mastership, and management over created things, excluding fellow humanity.

- **Purpose is the reason behind the creation of something.**

Nothing is ever created without a reason. Even if it was created for fun or beauty, it has a reason for it. Everything has a reason for its creation. And if we do not know the reason for its creation, it does not mean it has no reason because not every purpose is known. Even the butterfly, often admired for its colorful patterns, beauty, and graceful flight, uses them as symbolism for transformation and freedom, yet its reason for creation is to transfer pollen grains from one flower to another, allowing plants to produce seeds and fruits. This contributes to overall biodiversity and ecosystem balance. Most of us are ignorant about the purpose of a mosquito, often deeming its existence as bad, yet after creating every living creature, God said, *"And God saw that it was good" (Genesis 1:24).* It is because we are ignorant of its purpose. Mosquitoes serve as important members of ecosystems and food chains; they are a food source for organisms like birds, bats, and fish. Additionally, female mosquitoes play a role in pollination by feeding on nectar from flowers. Although mosquitoes may not align with our human desires, that does not nullify their purpose. Even the housefly, viewed as a disturbance by us, has a purpose in decomposition and nutrient recycling. They feed on decaying organic matter, such as garbage and excreta, helping break it down into simpler forms, contributing to the natural cycle of nutrient recycling in ecosystems. Although their purpose may not align with our desires due to the potential transmission of pathogens, their purpose remains.

Our facial hair, including beards and mustaches, serves as protection for the face, shielding it from direct sunlight, harsh weather conditions, and potential irritants. Although we may claim it for beauty purposes, that is not its reason for creation. Even the purpose of hips and buttocks, irrespective of their shape, size, or proportions, is not solely for dressing in a sexually provocative manner; they provide stability and balance during activities like walking, running, and sitting, and also contribute to easing fertility and childbirth in females. Even our nails, not primarily for aesthetics, assist in gripping and manipulating objects, facilitating fine motor skills.

Whenever we do not know the purpose of something, abuse tends to occur. This is why we witness instances of wife abuse, husband abuse, child abuse—all because we do not understand their purpose, leading to inevitable abuse where purpose is unknown.

The fact that people do not know, or you do not know the purpose of your life should not lead to abusing and distracting yourself with various pleasures. Your life holds meaning for this generation and has significance in this world. Being unaware of your purpose does not diminish your importance to your nation; they need you because there is a reason for your existence in that country. Once you re-discover your purpose for existence, you will experience disbelief because your belief system about yourself will start to unravel. You will grapple with your ideal self because you cannot believe in the "you" shaped by the grades the school system assigned to you or the yoke your culture placed on your neck, dictating beliefs about who you should be.

In other words, they control the diameter of your knowledge, which then dictates the circumference of your thinking about your possiblities. You were born with a purpose and for a purpose. Your purpose was not merely to be beautiful or handsome and rely on the fashion industry to enhance that status; there is more to it. Your beauty and handsomeness were perfect for your purpose, which is why you possess it. Your existence is not solely to showcase your beauty, handsomeness or to suck up air; there is something deeper to re-discover about what you were born to live for, my friend.

- **Purpose is the desired conclusion that the means are meant to bring about.**

God has already concluded everything about your life. Whatever is happening is not happening to you; it was meant to happen for you long ago, before your existence. Nothing has ever happened to you; it happened for you. Some of the things you are concerned about, God has already taken care of. That inner trauma you have been praying about, asking God to take away—it is already done. God saw what happened, what they did, who left you out, what you lost, the delays, the disappointments.

66

So, do not sit around in defeat, nursing your wounds. Do not ever put a question mark where God has put a period. We are never going to understand everything that happens. I know it was not fair, I know it was painful, but that is not your end; it was all a means to an end of God removing certain negative influences from your life. The company might say "you are fired," so they laid you off, but God says move on now because He is stripping everything away from you to bring you back to His purpose for you, to start your own business. God had already concluded your life before something happened for you, not to you.

You were already finished in God's mind before He brought you onto this planet. Just like constructors do not begin construction until they are already finished in their minds, the same thing happened to you; you were already finished in God's mind. When you request a permit to build your company, stall, worship center, house, the local government officials want to see the architectural plan that includes the electrical system, plumbing, roofing, and more. Essentially, they want to see everything finished—not only that but satisfied with your electrical system, plumbing, roofing that would not cause shocks, overflows, or leaks—before they give you their stamp of approval to start. Paul of Tarsus encapsulated this by putting it in these words:

> *"Praise be to the God and Father of our Lord Jesus Christ, who has blessed us in the heavenly realms with every spiritual blessing in Christ. For He chose us in Him before the creation of the world to be holy and blameless in His sight. In love, He predestined us to*

be adopted as His sons through Jesus Christ, in
accordance with His pleasure and will—to the praise
of His glorious grace, which He has freely given us in
the One He loves. In Him, we were also chosen, having
been predestined according to the plan of Him who
works out everything in conformity with the purpose of
His will [purpose]" (Ephesians 1:3-6,11).

This means, in effect, God has already concluded your life that caused Him to handpick you and decide to put you in a specific womb—that of your mother. You were God's concluded deepest desire, and He caused you to exist to fulfill something only you can do. You were predestined; thus, before you and I were born, God knew exactly our place on this planet Earth. He knows exactly where each of us would fit in.

He also says He *"works out everything in conformity with the purpose of His will [purpose]."* He says how many things? Everything—thus, all things—to fit into His purpose for your life. He did not say He will work out only the good things and the right things; He says everything, including all the bad breaks you have had, whatever you have messed up with, or failed at. He says He has figured out everything you are going through in conformity with His purpose for your life. That is, He works the means to the desired end He had purposed.

So, I challenge you to stop living under the grades they gave you based on the test you took some years ago. Having a failing moment does not mean you are a failure. Having bad days does not mean you are unlucky or a bad person. All these sorts of temptations that are coming to you are not demonically orchestrated; they were a training program laid down by God to get you back into His purpose for your life.

Nothing has ever happened to you that is more powerful than the purpose for your life. Everything was built as a plan—a means—to work into your purpose, thus to bring about the desired conclusion God has for your life. And I prophesy to you, that is a victorious one because you are not in the tomb, you are in the womb.

- **Purpose is the envisioned outcome that initiates the production process.**

Our God, the Creator of all things, including our lives, is a generational God. He is not confined to a narrow, bigoted secretariat group of people or an individual God. He operates generationally, thinking and acting in line with generations since the beginning of time. God foresaw the crises that would arise in your generation and prepared for it, making your existence necessary in this specific time in human history. The crises prevailing in your generation are not meant to conclude everything but to give credibility to your purpose. You were primarily born to solve these crisis issues.

Is it the rise of unemployment? Perhaps God is guiding you to turn that business idea in your mind into a reality now. Or maybe you were born to reform the education system in your country, tailoring studies to specific job skills. Is it the rise of immorality? Maybe you were born to embed God's laws and principles into your country's constitution. If you feel a personal obligation deep within your spirit, then you were born to address these crisis issues.

That is why whatever He purposed for your life is not solely for your benefit or that of the people in your lifetime. Your purpose serves the succeeding generations too. That is why He challenges you to think beyond your lifetime, prompting you to consider what legacy you wish to leave for the next generation. What do you want the succeeding generations to gain from your life at this phase on Earth?

Your purpose transcends your existence; it is meant to outlive you beyond the graveyard. It embodies an uncompromising eternalness of life. So, when death looms, you need not fear it, for your purpose was meant to live beyond you, only if you commit daily to its demands and fulfill them each day.

Your purpose was not solely for this generation. Hence, you owe it to leave something beneficial for succeeding generations. What legacy are you leaving for the next generation before taking your last breath?

- **Purpose is the need that necessitates a manufacturer to produce a specific product.**

There is something that needs to be done by God in this world to correct history that made your existence necessary. Without you, God will not do it, and without God, you cannot do it. You came into existence to address a challenge on Earth, serving as God's solution to a specific need He envisioned. You represent the response to a question that God foresaw would arise in your generation. Therefore, do not let anyone, any institution, or any circumstance diminish your sense of importance without your permission. You are importance because you are a solution to a problem in this world.

Moses solved the problem of oppression, David solved the problem of Goliath, Joseph solved the problem of dreams and economic crises, Daniel solved national administrative issues, Esther solved the problem of genocide, and Jesus Christ solved the problem of sin and death. That is why you should not ask God to remove every problem in your life. Behind some of the problems lie your greatness and wealth, just as Bill Gates, Elon Musk, Steve Jobs, Henry Ford solve specific problems in the world of 21st century and they became great and wealthy.

And if you never solve the problem you were born to solve, the problem still exists. That is why some of the problems that beat us here and there on this planet Earth are meant to be solved by the people in the graveyard now. Some of them even died poor because they could not identify the problem they were meant to solve, making this world the worst place to live.

The same applies to you; stop praying for deliverance from your greatness and wealth. When a problem shows up head-on that is meant to be solved by you, so do not ask God to remove it. The problem comes to introduce you to your purpose on Earth. You become great and wealthy based on the problem you solve in this world.

Problems create opportunities to meet yourself. They ignite the passion in you. Every problem that happens to you could be used to produce something beneficial to your generation and the succeeding ones. Your greatness and wealth lies behind the problem you were meant to solve. It is when facing problems that our creativity is born, and we get a new way of thinking about old problems. That is where inventions are born because inventions come out of a problem. Your existence is necessary for our world.

- **Purpose is the end result for setting out on a journey.**

Our God, the Creator of all things, is the God who never begins anything at the beginning. He begins everything at the end. In effect, He was the beginning before the beginning began, and whenever He begins something, that is proof that it is already finished. He always sets the end before the start. He finishes before He begins. Your end is already finished. Your purpose is already accomplished. That is why God is not worried about your future because, as far as He is concerned, it is already complete. He only lays down the plan for you to begin it. That is why your future is God's past. If you forget that your future is God's past and that He has already set out a victorious end for you, then you will experience depression, discouragement, lost momentum on your way there, and you will not even finish what you were born to start. You have to remember what God has said:

> "Remember this, fix it in mind, take it to heart, you
> rebels. Remember the former things, those of long ago;
> I am God, and there is no other; I am God, and there

is none like me. I make known the end from the beginning, from ancient times, what is still to come. I say: My purpose will stand, and I will do all that I please" (Isaiah 46:8-10).

In effect, God is saying, "let this foundational principle burn in your psyche, and do not rebel against Me by putting a full stop where I have placed a period." There is no god apart from our God who always finishes before He starts. He set your future as prosperous before He created you. Before your mother gave birth to you, He had already given you a purpose. God says that no matter what happens between where you are in life right now and when you will fulfill your purpose, all those things are temporary. He takes all of that and conforms it to the purpose He has given you, saying His purpose will stand.

To stand means it will prevail over everything, and nothing could destroy it, including the number of breakups or divorces you have had, the setbacks, the loss of some important people from your life, your health problems, the court issues you are facing right now, your mistakes, whether you have no job, bad grades, fail moments, or confinement in the four walls of prison cells. God still says He is working all things in conformity with the purpose of your life.

Nothing that you are facing or have been through could cancel your purpose. God has finished everything about your life, so relax and keep smiling at every phase of life because everything about your life that you are uncertain about, God is certain about, and He had already finished it. God is so sure and overconfidently wrote the end of the story of your life before the beginning.

- **Purpose is the intended expectation that the creator expects the created thing to fulfill.**

When God fashioned humanity, He expressed His intent: *"Then God said, 'Let Us make man in Our image, according to Our likeness; let them have dominion over the fish of the sea, over the birds of the air, and over the cattle, over all the earth and over every creeping thing that creeps on the earth'" (Genesis 1:26).*

In effect, God expects His created beings, us, humanity to dominate everything on Earth. Notice that nowhere was it stated that dominion extends over fellow human beings. God never intended for us to dominate ourselves. He specified what we humans were to have dominion over—thus, the creation and the earth. You were not designed to be dominated. That is why when you find yourself being dominated by another human being, there is this innate aspect of your human spirit that will urge you to throw off this unnatural restraint.

The concept of dominion relates to you, which includes ruling, managing, controlling, influencing, leading, governing, mastering, and having authority. This means anything that originates from the earth, whose raw materials come from the earth, is what you are meant to dominate. Your physical body came from the dirt of the earth, but it was not meant to dominate you as a spirit being. You are not your physical body; you are a spirit being, possessing a soul, residing in a physical body. Your spirit, as you were meant to, should dominate your physical body. So, if your physical body is dominating you as a spirit being, compelling you to indulge in drug abuse, theft, arrogance, a false sense of superiority, or promiscuity, do not walk around as if you have received some new revelation of life. You are too smart to be in that state. That is precisely a reversal of what your Creator God expects from you.

You were meant to dominate Earth, to put everything of it under control. You were born to be addicted to dominating the earth, not addicted to anything of the earth dominating you.

- **Purpose is the conviction of a vision that is created by inspiration, which becomes a passion for living.**

Purpose is inherent, and everything has an individual purpose that sets it apart, making it special, unique, and important in relation to others. Purpose is individual; every vision has only one initial believer, the person who has known their purpose. This individual becomes a believer to the extent that they know they were born solely to fulfill that purpose, hence called conviction. They begin to see that purpose conceptually, painting their future in the eyes of their mind. This is what makes most people who have re-discovered their purpose the most misunderstood in our world today. Their attitude arises from the re-discovery of their beliefs, where they believe nothing is impossible for them in what they set their hearts to achieve because they have become aware of their true abilities.

These people become more concerned with expressing themselves than proving themselves. They are so secure in the conviction of their visions that instead of proving themselves to others, they are more effective at being themselves. The vision they are convicted about is created by "inspiration," a concept originating from the Greek term meaning "divine deposit" or "god-breath." This means the source of their vision does not come from their culture or society; it comes from God, who gives purpose that provides a conceptual view of the purpose they were born to fulfill. In other words, purpose is an assignment with a devine touch.

These individuals are so convicted in the vision given to them by God that there is a break in ties with culture, believing that God's opinion about them is true, while others' opinions are lies. When I talk about "a break in ties with culture," it means a detachment from the collective thinking of their society. The person who knows their purpose and can envision it in their mind's eye no longer believes in what their society calls "normal"; they see it as "mediocrity." They believe in the untested and the unattempted and always strive to do the impossible, regardless of the intellectual, philosophical, religious, or scientific barriers experts may present.

These individuals have declared independence from other people's expectations and will never allow others to determine who they should become. They stand out so effectively that their position cannot be corrected to fit in; they are always at the right position that cannot be adjusted. We label them as anti-social, difficult people who disrupt traditions, break cultural boundaries, and pose questions that are unnecessary that the world cannot even answer.

The vision they see through their mind's eye, created by "divine deposit" or "god-breath," becomes their passion for living. They genuinely believe that divinity has chosen them to do something special that no one else can do, something they would even die for because it is worth sacrificing their lives for.

It is my hope that you will be inspired to respond to the call of purpose and commit to fulfilling it. Your season has arrived, but you should focus on studying yourself to know and be convicted about the life you were meant to live, a life worth dying for.

Chapter 3: Principles To Think About Before You Take Your Last Breath

———

1. The deepest yearning of the human spirit is to attain a sense of ultimate fulfillment. The pursuit of this ultimate fulfillment in life stands as humanity's paramount pursuit. Not a single soul on Earth desires to endure unending suffering, frustration, anxiety, depression, or inner trauma. We all strive to discover this profound sense of contentment within ourselves.

2. It is important to realize that your life's fulfillment hinges upon recapturing the meaning of existence for your life—termed "purpose"—and ardently pursuing it with unwavering commitment. Anything less would render life an adversary and death a companion.

3. Success lies in fulfilling one's purpose, adhering to its dictates. Therefore, success can solely be defined by purpose and gauged by one's commitment to it.

4. Fulfillment only materializes when purpose is re-captured and lived out.

5. Purpose represents the original idea behind creating something, existing in the mind of its creator. It essentially embodies the "why" in the creator's mind. This principle is fundamental in the manufacturing world, never skipped by any manufacturer. No manufacturer creates a product and then decides to

discover its purpose through experimentation afterward. Essentially, before a product materializes, its purpose already exists in the creator's mind as an idea.

6. Purpose precedes creation, residing solely in the mind of the creator. Finding the purpose of a thing involves seeking it from the creator of the thing.

7. Purpose is not an afterthought or an external layer added to things. Instead, it stands as an integral and inherent aspect of what a thing is. It is the natural makeup, the DNA, if you will, of every entity in existence. Purpose is not a skill acquired or a trait learned; it is innate, existing from the very moment of creation.

8. Purpose, therefore, cannot be discovered in the conventional sense; it can only be re-discovered. It is not a puzzle waiting to be solved but a fundamental aspect waiting to be acknowledged.

9. The purposes of our lives are not something we create; instead, we have the opportunity to re-capture them. Like a hidden treasure waiting to be unearthed, purpose comes with the product, inherent in our existence, not external to it.

10. Just as a tree bears fruits according to its kind, so does purpose manifest in alignment with the essence of the created thing. It is not a transient companion that can be abandoned at will; it is an inseparable companion woven into the very fabric of existence.

11. Understanding why something exists or was created helps us comprehend what is supposed to do it and

how it is supposed to operate or work.

12. Purpose becomes the guiding factor that shapes the entire design process.

13. Knowing your purpose serves as a filter for decision-making. It helps you discern where to be, the kind of people to surround yourself with, and the paths to tread or avoid. It acts as a protective barrier, steering you away from actions that might jeopardize your well-being or hinder your growth.

14. The purpose of a thing determines its inherent capabilities. This implies that the design and function of a thing play a crucial role in defining its effectiveness and possibilities.

15. Success, when measured through the lens of purpose, is not just about reaching a destination but also about the journey itself.

16. Our purpose acts as a lens through which we view our future. It provides clarity and direction, helping us prioritize our goals and make decisions aligned with our values. Without a clear purpose, our vision might be blurry or undefined, making it challenging to work towards specific objectives.

17. Purpose maintains objectivity by anchoring us to the intended function of things, steering us away from subjective interpretations or arbitrary applications. It upholds the integrity of objects, ensuring they remain true to their essence and function.

18. The essence of measuring life's value lies not in the duration it exists, but rather in the fulfillment of its intended purpose. Think of it this way: the

significance of a life is not solely determined by how long it lasts, but by the impact it makes through achieving its intended goals.

19. The measure of a life well-lived lies in the alignment of actions, choices, and efforts with one's purpose. It is about making the most of the time one has by investing it in endeavors that resonate with their deepest aspirations, values, and convictions. In doing so, individuals create a legacy that extends beyond their years, graveyard and continues to impact the world. In effect, the true measure of life is not the number of years lived, but the extent to which one lives with purpose, contributing meaningfully to the world around them.

20. Only God, the Creator of your life, knows the original idea for our creation. Anyone apart from God is merely guessing, experimenting, presuming, or assuming our purpose, and despite their sincere attempts—whether psychologically, philosophically, biologically, or theologically—they can be faithfully wrong if not authorized with God's original idea for our lives. That is why nothing is worst than being sincere about something and be faithfully wrong. Because being sincere does not mean you are right, you can be faithfully wrong about that thing.

21. Jesus Christ is God's original idea on two legs, thus in human form. Therefore, you should turn to Jesus Christ not to embrace a religion or confine yourself to narrow church meetings, but to re-discover the life you were born to live. Hence, one of His famous

statements is, "I am the Way, the Truth, and the Life. No one comes to the Father (God) except through Me" (John 14:6). In other words, Jesus Christ asserts that He is the only authorized person (the Way) who knows God's original idea (the Truth) about your existence (the Life). And if you still doubt that He is the only one who knows the purpose for your life, Jesus Christ reveals that God, the Creator of your life, has made Him the only person who can guide you to reach Him, "...No one comes to the Father (God) except through Me." That is deep!

22. Purpose is inherent in creation because it is built into creation, not what you try to make it be. Therefore, you cannot monetary, intellectually, awakeningly, or spiritually create your own purpose for life.

23. The purpose of humanity is not created by humans, it is re-discovered to live it by humans. If what you are doing dominates you, it is a sign that it is not your destined path on Earth. You were inherently designed for rulership, leadership, influence, impact, mastership, and management over created things, excluding fellow humanity.

24. Nothing is ever created without a reason. Even if it was created for fun or beauty, it has a reason for it. Everything has a reason for its creation. And if we do not know the reason for its creation, it does not mean it has no reason because not every purpose is known.

25. The fact that people do not know, or you do not know the purpose of your life should not lead to abusing and distracting yourself with various pleasures. Your

life holds meaning for this generation and has significance in this world. Being unaware of your purpose does not diminish your importance to your nation; they need you because there is a reason for your existence in that country. Once you re-discover your purpose for existence, you will experience disbelief because your belief system about yourself will start to unravel. You will grapple with your ideal self because you cannot believe in the "you" shaped by the grades the school system assigned to you or the yoke your culture placed on your neck, dictating beliefs about who you should be.

26. You were born with a purpose and for a purpose. Your purpose was not merely to be beautiful or handsome and rely on the fashion industry to enhance that status; there is more to it. Your beauty and handsomeness were perfect for your purpose, which is why you possess it. Your existence is not solely to showcase your beauty, handsomeness or to suck up air; there is something deeper to re-discover about what you were born to live for, my friend.

27. God has already concluded everything about your life. Whatever is happening is not happening to you; it was meant to happen for you long ago, before your existence. Nothing has ever happened to you; it happened for you. Some of the things you are concerned about, God has already taken care of. That inner trauma you have been praying about, asking God to take away—it is already done. God saw what happened, what they did, who left you out, what you

lost, the delays, the disappointments.

28. Do not sit around in defeat, nursing your wounds. Do not ever put a question mark where God has put a period. We are never going to understand everything that happens. I know it was not fair, I know it was painful, but that is not your end; it was all a means to an end of God removing certain negative influences from your life. The company might say "you are fired," so they laid you off, but God says move on now because He is stripping everything away from you to bring you back to His purpose for you, to start your own business. God had already concluded your life before something happened for you, not to you.

29. God has already concluded your life that caused Him to handpick you and decide to put you in a specific womb—that of your mother. You were God's concluded deepest desire, and He caused you to exist to fulfill something only you can do. You were predestined; thus, before you and I were born, God knew exactly our place on this planet Earth. He knows exactly where each of us would fit in.

30. Having a failing moment does not mean you are a failure. Having bad days does not mean you are unlucky or a bad person. All these sorts of temptations that are coming to you are not demonically orchestrated; they were a training program laid down by God to get you back into His purpose for your life.

31. Nothing has ever happened to you that is more powerful than the purpose for your life. Everything was built as a plan—a means—to work into your

purpose, thus to bring about the desired conclusion God has for your life. And I prophesy to you, that is a victorious one because you are not in the tomb, you are in the womb.

32. When death looms, you need not fear it, for your purpose was meant to live beyond you, only if you commit daily to its demands and fulfill them each day.

33. There is something that needs to be done by God in this world to correct history that made your existence necessary. Without you, God will not do it, and without God, you cannot do it. You came into existence to address a challenge on Earth, serving as God's solution to a specific need He envisioned. You represent the response to a question that God foresaw would arise in your generation. Therefore, do not let anyone, any institution, or any circumstance diminish your sense of importance without your permission. You are importance because you are a solution to a problem in this world.

34. Your greatness and wealth lies behind the problem you were meant to solve.

35. Our God, the Creator of all things, is the God who never begins anything at the beginning. He begins everything at the end. In effect, He was the beginning before the beginning began, and whenever He begins something, that is proof that it is already finished. He always sets the end before the start. He finishes before He begins. Your end is already finished. Your purpose is already accomplished. That is why God is not worried about your future because, as far as He is

concerned, it is already complete. He only lays down the plan for you to begin it. That is why your future is God's past. If you forget that your future is God's past and that He has already set out a victorious end for you, then you will experience depression, discouragement, lost momentum on your way there, and you will not even finish what you were born to start.

36. Nothing that you are facing or have been through could cancel your purpose. God has finished everything about your life, so relax and keep smiling at every phase of life because everything about your life that you are uncertain about, God is certain about, and He had already finished it. God is so sure and overconfidently wrote the end of the story of your life before the beginning.

37. You were meant to dominate Earth, to put everything of it under control. You were born to be addicted to dominating the earth, not addicted to anything of the earth dominating you.

38. Your season has arrived, but you should focus on studying yourself to know and be convicted about the life you were meant to live, a life worth dying for.

CHAPTER

4

Understanding The Fundamental Nature Of The Meaning Of Existence For Your Life

———

The surest way to mess up your life is by delving into every subject imaginable, except the most important one – yourself. In a world that constantly emphasizes the significance of external achievements, it is easy to lose sight of the internal journey. We consume vast amounts of information on how to influence, attract, and understand others, neglecting the essential task of understanding ourselves. The focal point of a truly fulfilling life is self-awareness – knowing who you are, understanding your purpose, and living authentically.

Contrary to popular belief, the pursuit of fulfillment is not a journey outward but an exploration inward. External factors such as job titles, academic credentials, or relationship status may offer temporary satisfaction, but fulfilment stems from aligning your life with your unique purpose. Fulfillment is not about imitating others; it is about re-discovering, understanding, committing to, and passionately living out your individual purpose.

The pages of this book serve as a guide to unravel the essence of your existence on this planet Earth. The purpose for your life is an intricate dance with your true self, a dance orchestrated by the Creator of all things, God. It transcends societal norms and encourages embracing your evolving self, driven by an unwavering passion for your purpose.

As you immerse yourself in the wisdom shared within these pages, you will come to the profound realization that fulfillment starts from understanding the fundamental nature of the meaning of existence for your life. This will help us gain in-depth knowledge of the meaning of our existence. Our purpose is the end that started the beginning, the finish before the start, the destination before the journey, the final address for our lives, and the reason for our birth. Let us begin our exploration of the fundamental nature of the purpose for our lives.

- **Purpose is a universal principle.**

Purpose is a fundamental concept that applies universally. Everything possesses a specific reason for its existence. In simpler terms, nothing comes into being without a purpose behind its creation. This principle is observable in nature, where every living being, including each one of us, has been purposed by God, the Creator of all things, to fulfill His plan. We all participate in this overarching principle of purpose, and no one is exempt from God's intention. Every individual on Earth is chosen by God to contribute to His grand plan, as stated in Ephesians 1:11:

> *"In Him we were chosen, having been predestined according to the plan of Him who works out everything in conformity with the purpose of His will."*

Regardless of how your life began or the challenges you may have faced, you are not a mistake; your purpose was predetermined before your earthly journey commenced. God intended for you to live in this specific generation and in the world as it exists today. Your birth was not a random event; rather, it was a deliberate inclusion in God's plan for the era and age in which you currently reside. You are not only a product of God's plan but also necessary and very important to your community.

The universality of purpose provides a comforting anchor when life seems devoid of meaning or value. It assures us that we are not accidental beings, and our existence, whether in a remote location, by a water body, in a hospital, prison, workplace, school, detained area, or any other setting, is part of God's intentional plan.

This understanding grants us significance, affirming that our presence is not a mere coincidence but a deliberate inclusion in the unfolding narrative of God's plan. Embracing the idea that God has intricately planned our existence helps us find solace and purpose in the most challenging circumstances. It underscores the belief that, regardless of our current situation, we are integral to God's scheme of things.

In essence, this perspective encourages a sense of responsibility and accountability. If we acknowledge that our lives are intricately linked to God's plan, it compels us to live with intentionality and contribute positively to the world around us. Recognizing the universality of purpose fosters a deeper connection with our Creator, God and a greater understanding of our function in the grand tapestry of existence.

- **Purpose is inherent.**

You did not acquire a purpose or "a calling" for your life by joining a spiritual movement. Your purpose for existence was not bestowed upon you when you became religiously committed. Your purpose existed before your birth, accompanying you from the moment you landed in your mother's womb as a sperm, transforming into a zygote, then a fetus, and eventually into a baby.

Your purpose is both natural and physical, not something obtained through monetary transactions or ritualistic activities. Your inherent attributes, such as height, race, skin color, language, physical features, and intellectual capacity, are all designed to fulfill your purpose.

It is crucial not to confuse religious roles with your life's purpose. Your life extends beyond rituals and specific practices. Your role is something you choose to do and can quit, but your purpose is inseparable, inherent. Deciding to live without it may lead to self-frustration. Your purpose is not achieved through prayer, meditation, or work; it is innate, born with you. In effect, purpose is built into creation.

- **Purpose is particular.**

You were born to be known for one thing, and what you were born to be known for, no one on Earth can substitute you for that. You were not born to be known for everything. God made your birth necessary for you to be a master of one thing on this planet Earth. This is what makes your absence felt even when you take your last breath into the graveyard.

What you were born to be known for is what opens doors for you, not only that, but it also makes you popular and important to us, humanity. Whether you become "well-known" in the entire known world is not an issue; your only concern is to re-discover your purpose for existence and start becoming it, because your purpose is something you become by fulfilling or doing it.

Many people pursue popularity or fame, but they have forgotten that if it is not grounded in purpose, it is like a "flame" that will just go out one day. People will walk past you and not even recognize that you were that guy who used to trend some moments in human history. Instead, people should pursue becoming what they were born to be known for, and their popularity or fame will never go out. They will recognize that when they do that, popularity or fame will not only chase them on the road of becoming themselves, but prosperity will come towards them head-on. Our prosperity is found in what we were born to be known for. So do not allow the normality of the culture of your society to pressure you into being known for everything on the premises of what the majority pursues. Know what you were born to be known for, and when you re-discover it, do not stray from becoming it.

Every person on Earth exists to be known for one particular thing, and the world pays you for becoming it by doing it. That is why people mostly become great after they die because they were too effective dying from the world's expectations of them before they even die. They die becoming what they were born to be known for by doing it, and that is why too their absence on this planet is much felt than when they were alive.

- **Purpose is interrelated.**

Imagine if oxygen existed without carbon dioxide. Imagine having only teeth in your mouth but no tongue. Imagine if there were only one gender of sex in existence. Everything exists for one another, not for itself. That is why you must crush your ego and kill the pride inside you, if you think you are the only important person in your workplace, school, or religion, or anywhere you find yourself. And if you are thinking like that, then you have not connected with reality yet.

Realize there is nobody named "stupid," "idiot," "foolish," "mad," "unnecessary," or "unimportant." Everybody is important, including you. Just because others do not see your importance does not mean you should harm yourself with destructive behaviors. Your importance comes from God, not social status, job, salary, qualifications, or whether you get none of them. Remember, as long as you do not succumb to suicide, you are important.

The thing is most good people are blind on the premise of seeing the importance of others; do not label what God called "good" as bad. It is circumstances that lead people to destructive behavior; never call what God deems good as bad.

Nothing on Earth exists for itself; everything exists for one another. Even the housefly exists to decompose waste matter, contributing to soil fertility. Consider the purpose of kids in children's homes and those society deems "mad"; they too have importance. Everyone is significant in some way; do not dismiss your importance or that of others.

Your birth was necessary for a reason, to live for others and for them to live for others including you. Fulfilling your purpose requires interconnected contributions, according to God's plan. Do not let examination scores cancel out your importance; contribute to making the world better.

Your existence matters; you fulfilling your purpose can awaken dormant potential in others. You need others and others need you too on your journey to fulfilling your purpose. The world awaits your commitment to fulfilling your purpose. Everyone is important, interrelated in God's plan, canceling out inferiority and superiority.

- **Purpose is equipped.**

God has equipped everything with the potential to fulfill its purpose. In life, each element possesses the potential to fulfill its existence. This potential resides within, as seen in a seed's ability to grow into a tree or a fish's ability to swim. Similarly, your eyes inherently hold the potential for sight. A creation's potential is never external to it or within the Creator; it is inherent.

You are "self-sufficient" with an inborn purpose and built-in potentials to fulfill it. Your potential encompasses unused talents, hidden skills, unexposed gifts, and untapped power to become who you have not yet been. Paul of Tarsus captured this potential's source, stating,

> *"Now to Him Who, by (in consequence of) the [action of His] power that is at work within us, is able to [carry out His purpose and] do superabundantly, far over and above all that we [dare] ask or think [infinitely beyond our highest prayers, desires, thoughts, hopes, or dreams]" (Ephesians 3:20).*

This power, described as *within us*, dispels the notion of impossibility. Your potential is not contingent on external factors like rituals, prayers, education, prison cells, sick bed, or any circumstances. The power to fulfill your purpose is within you, transcending any external influence. Embrace the conviction that God never assigns a purpose without providing the power to fulfill it. The power resides within you, surpassing any external forces. Never give up that power within by thinking that you have none.

Recognize that the power within you is greater than that outside you. Do not let external circumstances dictate your potential; instead, use the power within to influence your surroundings. Refuse to submit to past or present challenges; you possess the capability to surpass expectations. Because the Bible says, God's power with you will succeed and exceed your prayers, desires, thoughts, hopes, or dreams.

Be effective, not busy in life, tapping into your hidden potential. Strive for greatness, breaking barriers, setting trends, and leaving a legacy of impossibilities for your generation and the future generations.

- **Purpose is permanent.**

Nothing is unstoppable as change. Change is everywhere. Change does not stop when we sleep, take a vacation, or go on a lunch break. Change is continual. Everything in this world will change.

Your interests in certain things you love will change. Your relationships with certain people will change. The value that people hold dear to your heart will change. Your job may change. Your knowledge will change. Your body features will change. Your family relationships network will change. Situations may cause people you are in a relationship with to undergo change. The universe that forces certain people into your life will force some out of your life; your friends will change. Change is inevitable.

No one on Earth can avoid change. This conclusion is not easy for some people to accept. Life is full of the unexpected, and changes will come upon us at some time or another. Wealth, title, intelligence, popularity, success, good intentions, great anointing, meditations, or prayers do not make you immune. No matter who you are, you will experience it. So, whenever you encounter change—especially change you consider disruptive or distressing—do not feel like you are all alone in this. We are all subject to change! But nothing is more unchangeable as the purpose for your life, given to you by God, the Creator of all things.

> Men swear by someone greater than themselves, and the oath confirms what is said and puts an end to all argument. Because **God wanted to make the unchanging nature of His purpose very clear** to the heirs of what was promised, He confirmed it with an oath" (Hebrews 6:16-17).

Life's promise lies in the paradox that everything in your life will shift according to your purpose for existence. Life is designed to evolve, not stay stagnant. Re-discovering God's purposes for us, seeking His guidance, and understanding what comes next are essential. This prevents being overwhelmed by the present on the journey to the future. While life may seem unpredictable to us, to God, it steadily progresses toward fulfilling His ultimate plan.

Being ready for any possibility eases the impact of change, knowing that God is with us through every transformation. Just like Abraham, who had to leave his homeland to become the father of nations, and Joseph, who faced loss before rising to prominence, life's changes are part of the process. Clinging to God's nature and purposes amid transitions ensures a safe arrival at the destination He intended—which does not change. God encourages us to embrace change, as depicted in Isaiah 43:18-19:

"Forget the former things; do not dwell on the past. See, I am doing a new thing!"

Staying connected to God through prayer and His Word helps navigate life's changes without feeling overwhelmed. God's purpose for our lives remains permanent, change were meant though to elevate our thinking that there is something for our lives. Understanding that everything in our lives will change provides relief from the pressure to maintain the status quo. Life's surprises become less bewildering when we accept that it does not follow a predefined pattern.

Embrace change, knowing it prepares you for your purpose which is permanent, even if the bigger picture remains unseen. Your purpose remains unchanged; it is constant, shaping everything around it. Always move forward, as life unfolds in that direction, and remember, understanding comes in hindsight. Never worship your past, appreciate your present, and take responsibility for your future.

- **Purpose is self-fulfilling.**

Each person on Earth has a unique purpose crafted by God's plan, and this purpose is inherently self-fulfilling. However, societal norms discourage self-promotion, leading us to downplay our importance and shy away from self-confidence. Our culture often labels self-assuredness as selfishness, ingraining a belief that we should fit in rather than stand out.

This societal conditioning leaves us hesitant to boldly proclaim, "I was born for this purpose, and the world needs my contribution." This disconnection from our selves hinders our ability to recognize and embrace our purposes. We become so consumed with fitting in that we neglect the opportunity to stand out. The fear of being perceived as selfish or egotistical prevents us from fully believing in our unique visions.

In essence, we have been conditioned to fear our visions as they represent a glimpse into our potential future, an image of what we could become. Our visions are like a photograph of our endpoint, and we have been taught to be apprehensive about them. The key, however, is to view our visions as our future addresses and appreciate them as integral parts of our identities.

When someone grasps the vision of their existence on this planet, they prioritize their future over their past, fostering a deep appreciation for the present. Passion then takes center stage, becoming a force stronger than death. This passion propels individuals to not only live for their purpose but also be willing to die for it, marking the reclamation of the true purpose of their lives.

Passion transforms individuals into unstoppable forces. The purpose woven into our lives is designed to test us, demanding belief and commitment. Much like an eaglet pushed off a cliff, hitting rocks on the way down, only to be picked up again by its mother and pushed out once more until it conquers the fear and learns to fly. The journey involves facing failures and embracing opportunities, ultimately realizing the destiny to become what they initially doubted.

It is important not to let societal influences dissuade personal growth. Those who have left a mark in history had to declare independence from societal expectations, often adopting the label of a rebel. Rebels defy prescribed norms and reject the need for approval, because they have found something more important than that—thus, the meaning of existence for their lives.

God, according to Jeremiah 1:12, is actively watching to ensure the fulfillment of His purpose in our lives. Thus, there is no need to panic about the challenges and visions in our minds. If the vision is uniquely seen by us, it is evidence that we are meant to fulfill it. The time to act is now, without waiting for external validation or the perfect moment. Start before you feel you are ready, as the journey towards fulfilling your purpose begins with taking the first step.

- **Purpose can be unknown.**

Re-discovering one's purpose is important; without it, life becomes a void, devoid of meaning, leading to a path of emptiness, destruction, and mere survival. Moses, initially seeing himself as a shepherd, encounters God, the Creator of all things, who unveils Moses' purpose – as a deliverer and the author of the first five books of the Bible. God designates Moses as a lawgiver for all nations. Moses, taken aback, doubts this calling.

Similarly, many fear embracing their selves due to societal expectations and internal conflicts. Gideon, initially cowering in fear, is told by God that he is a mighty man of valor. Yet, Gideon, shackled by self-doubt, questions God's message, attributing his background as unsuitable for such valor. Gideon sets up a test, demonstrating the common human tendency to argue with our selves, hoping for a sign that aligns with our preconceived notions.

The pervasive fear of embracing one's purpose stems from societal influences and personal insecurities. People often engage in internal debates, convincing themselves that their intended purpose is incompatible with their circumstances or background. Gideon's reluctance mirrors this struggle, as he grapples with societal expectations and self-imposed limitations.

The quest for purpose is hindered by the pervasive influence of external opinions, cultural norms, and personal expectations. Gideon's hesitation to accept his identity exemplifies the internal conflict many face when confronted with their purpose. The external world's standards often clash with the authentic self, leading to a perpetual state of inner turmoil.

The concept that life lacks purpose merely because one cannot immediately discern it is challenged. Not every purpose is known from the outset; re-discovery becomes important. I, Mfoamfo passionately contends that no individual should depart this Earth without re-capturing their life's purpose. The anger in my heart underscores the urgency of this revelation that every person has a unique purpose waiting to be uncovered.

Distractions, whether external or internal, are to be resisted on the journey to self-recapturing. The assurance is given that everyone is born with a purpose that transcends an empty, meaningless, and destructive existence. Re-discovering this purpose becomes transformative, nullifying the list of detrimental outcomes and transforming every day into a meaningful journey. Living in alignment with one's purpose results in a life grounded in passion, making each day a play day.

- **Purpose has a timeframe in which it is carried out and completed.**

"To everything there is a season, a time for every purpose under heaven" (Ecclesiastes 3:1). These words re-capture the spirit that we were not born to live forever. The word "season" is often used to define change that is not a short-term event but rather an extended period of transition, indicating the non-permanent nature of our conditions in time and assuring us that nothing remains the same. That is why we should never measure our lives by our present condition, but by the condition of what we see in the eyes of our minds because that is exactly where we are going.

Everything is "seasonal" within a limited time frame. Everything that is created—everything that is below the invisible, eternal realm of God—exists in time. Everything that exists in time has a purpose, and each of these purposes has a time for its fulfillment. All humans exist in time; time is a piece of eternity with a beginning and an end. As long as your life began, it has to end someday.

The most powerful tribe in ancient Israel was not Judah; it was Issachar. Why? Because they understood the times and therefore knew what Israel should do (1 Chronicles 12:32, emphasis added). The tribe of Issachar was large and had many men who were able to fight. Yet it was not their size or strength that made them powerful; it was their capacity to understand the times in which they lived. They knew what was happening in their environment, they could interpret the conditions, and therefore they could project for the whole nation what it should do. This is the reason why receiving prophecy from God was so important in the context of the national life of the ancient Israelites.

The most ideal human who ever lived was Jesus Christ because He had a clear picture of His purpose for existence in the eyes of His mind; He knew what He should be doing at any given moment. Jesus Christ was the only human being who lived effectively on this planet Earth without getting busy because He knew why He was here on this planet and therefore what He should be doing within thirty-three years of His existence on Earth. He understood that whoever controls and manages your time controls your experience in time; not only that but also literally designs your future.

One day during a festive season in Jesus Christ's childhood, His earthly parents were searching for Him and He was nowhere to be found. When they found Him at the temple sitting with some religious scholars who understood the scriptures and could even tell you the meaning and historical essence of each word in a sentence, His parents asked Him to go back home with them. This is what Jesus Christ said to His earthly parents, *"Did you know that I must be about My Father's work?" (Luke 2:49, emphasis added).* He was saying, in effect, "I have been with you for twelve years already and you still do not know why I am here on Earth and what I should be doing by now."

Can I tell you, friend, that your mother, who carried you for nine months, does not know the times you are in now and what you should be doing? Your father does not even know your purpose for existence on this planet; that is why he could be dictating what you should do with your life, impressing you with good intellectual reasons on why you should pursue certain areas of study in school, and deep in your human spirit you knew he is sincerely wrong about you.

You should understand where you are now and what you should be doing with your life now. Do not get busy with life, be effective because nothing is more barren than a busy life. And if you do not have parents, it does not matter; it is about you, not about your parents. You do not have a father? So what! You do not know your mother? Do not worry. You are here on Earth and you are dearly welcome. Let us make an impact to transform the world for better before we die by understanding the times and what we ought to do based on our purpose.

One day, Jesus Christ and His disciples were invited to a wedding at Cana in Galilee. Jesus Christ's mother was there, and when the wine was gone, she said to Him, "They have no more wine." Jesus Christ replied, *"My time has not yet come"* *(John 2:4)*. Friend, if you do not understand the time you are living in, you will be doing the good thing but not the right thing.

John the Baptist was born to be *"A voice of one calling in the desert, 'Prepare the way for the Lord, make straight paths for Him [Jesus Christ]'" (Matthew 3:3)*. That was the purpose of his life.

John was born to introduce Jesus Christ to the world when Jesus Christ was thirty years old, and after he had introduced Jesus Christ, that was exactly the completion of his purpose for existence on this planet Earth, and also the commencement of Jesus Christ's purpose. Notice what happened when he was done with his purpose for introducing Jesus Christ to the world; he was detained in prison and he was confused. So he sent some of his disciples to go and ask Jesus if He really was the Messiah or Christ that he, John the Baptist, introduced. Jesus Christ's reply was, *"Go back and report to John what you hear and see: The blind receive sight, the lame walk, those who have leprosy are cured, the deaf hear, the dead are raised, and the good news is preached to the poor. Blessed is the man who does not fall away on account of Me" (Matthew 11:4-6)*. Once John's purpose on Earth for introducing Jesus as the Christ was completed, he was beheaded.

Can I tell you that it is your purpose that is keeping you alive? There is something you alone were born to do that the whole Heaven is backing you up to complete because there is a timeframe for it to be carried out and completed. It is your purpose that is protecting you from untimely death. Once the timeframe set for its completion reaches you just die because you were not born to live forever; you were born to live in time.

Chapter 4: Principles To Think About Before You Take Your Last Breath

———

1. The surest way to mess up your life is by delving into every subject imaginable, except the most important one – yourself. In a world that constantly emphasizes the significance of external achievements, it is easy to lose sight of the internal journey. We consume vast amounts of information on how to influence, attract, and understand others, neglecting the essential task of understanding ourselves. The focal point of a truly fulfilling life is self-awareness – knowing who you are, understanding your purpose, and living authentically.

2. Regardless of how your life began or the challenges you may have faced, you are not a mistake; your purpose was predetermined before your earthly journey commenced. God intended for you to live in this specific generation and in the world as it exists today. Your birth was not a random event; rather, it was a deliberate inclusion in God's plan for the era and age in which you currently reside. You are not only a product of God's plan but also necessary and very important to your community.

3. You did not acquire a purpose or "a calling" for your life by joining a spiritual movement. Your purpose for existence was not bestowed upon you when you

became religiously committed. Your purpose existed before your birth, accompanying you from the moment you landed in your mother's womb as a sperm, transforming into a zygote, then a fetus, and eventually into a baby.

4. Your purpose is both natural and physical, not something obtained through monetary transactions or ritualistic activities. Your inherent attributes, such as height, race, skin color, language, physical features, and intellectual capacity, are all designed to fulfill your purpose.

5. You were born to be known for one thing, and what you were born to be known for, no one on Earth can substitute you for that. You were not born to be known for everything. God made your birth necessary for you to be a master of one thing on this planet Earth. This is what makes your absence felt even when you take your last breath into the graveyard.

6. Know what you were born to be known for, and when you re-discover it, do not stray from becoming it.

7. Your existence matters; you fulfilling your purpose can awaken dormant potential in others. You need others and others need you too on your journey to fulfilling your purpose. The world awaits your commitment to fulfilling your purpose. Everyone is important, interrelated in God's plan, canceling out inferiority and superiority.

8. You are "self-sufficient" with an inborn purpose and built-in potentials to fulfill it. Your potential encompasses unused talents, hidden skills, unexposed

gifts, and untapped power to become who you have not yet been.

9. Embrace the conviction that God never assigns a purpose without providing the power to fulfill it. The power resides within you, surpassing any external forces. Never give up that power within by thinking that you have none.

10. Be effective, not busy in life, tapping into your hidden potential. Strive for greatness, breaking barriers, setting trends, and leaving a legacy of impossibilities for your generation and the future generations.

11. Nothing is more unchangeable as the purpose for your life. Life's promise lies in the paradox that everything in your life will shift according to your purpose for existence.

12. Always move forward, as life unfolds in that direction, and remember, understanding comes in hindsight. Never worship your past, appreciate your present, and take responsibility for your future.

13. Rebels defy prescribed norms and reject the need for approval, because they have found something more important than that—thus, the meaning of existence for their lives.

14. Start before you feel you are ready.

15. Living in alignment with one's purpose results in a life grounded in passion, making each day a play day.

16. We should never measure our lives by our present condition, but by the condition of what we see in the eyes of our minds because that is exactly where we are going.

17. All humans exist in time; time is a piece of eternity with a beginning and an end. As long as your life began, it has to end someday.

18. Whoever controls and manages your time controls your experience in time; not only that but also literally designs your future.

19. Do not get busy with life, be effective because nothing is more barren than a busy life.

20. You were not born to live forever; you were born to live in time.

CHAPTER

5

On Becoming Yourself

———

B ecoming yourself is a monumental achievement in a world constantly pushing you to conform. Trusting yourself is key—do not yield to societal pressures that conflict with what you sees in the eyes of your mind—vision. Do not carry guilt for not meeting others' expectations; focus on fulfilling your unique life purpose. You are not here to follow religious or school paths forced upon you by others; embrace your authenticity.

Some people regretfully say, "I didn't want to become this." They have faced inner conflicts, conforming to societal expectations, and devaluing themselves to fit into the world's mold. But you, my friend, do not need to devalue yourself for acceptance. Be authentic; if others cannot appreciate it, move forward. You do not require validation to become who God intended you to be. Do not worry about being by doing it perfectly now; progress matters. In time, you will settle into yourself, grateful you did not conform.

God, the Creator of all things, presents moments in our lives where our instincts defy logic, upsetting plans and appearing meaningless to others. In those times, listen to your instincts because it is back up with the entire nation of Heaven, ignoring logic, odds, and complications—just do it. Refrain from conforming to societal expectations that lead to self-criticism.

It is time to stop fitting in; accept your limitless potential to stand out. Recognize your greatness as it comes to view.

God cancel out your plans to save you from dangers. Give thanks to God for rejection, redirection, and realization. God fights battles unknown to you, with plans superior to yours. Regardless of the moment, realize you are always moving towards magnificence by God's plan. Do not convince yourself it is too late to begin; start now, for God's timing is never too late.

The real battles are not for breaking Guinea World Records; it is breaking free from world's expectations. Living according to the world's expectations makes us lose ourselves, pleasing others at the expense of authenticity. People offer condolences in death but disrupt your peace while alive, only to pray for your rest in peace after you are gone. Ironically, I congratulate the dead; they remain true to themselves.

Never forget that nobody can live your life's purpose for you. They do not even know it, nor your potential, so do not let them question your abilities. When God paints a picture in your mind, do not dismiss it; it holds power to change your life. Do not hold back due to fear; your best work comes after embracing your worst attempts. Fear of failure often prevents greatness, as many fear attempting things they could succeed at.

Ignore the world's priorities; ask yourself about God's priorities, that is what makes you come alive. The clock is ticking, but it is never too late on God's clock. Reconnect with yourself before the past overshadows the future. Have a meeting with yourself as you continue to read the pages of this book backed by a divine touch from God, embrace who you are, fulfill your purpose, and let your authentic self shine brightly before you take your last breath.

RE-UNDERSTANDING THE PRIORITIES OF GOD FOR YOUR LIFE

In the heart of every person lies a deep desire for a simple life. We naturally gravitate towards those who lead purposeful, focused, and organized lives. This inclination towards simplicity is, in my view, the underlying reason why countless individuals are drawn to Jesus Christ. His character uniquely embodied qualities like personal conviction, vision, passion, self-awareness, confidence, self-worth, and a clear sense of destiny. What set Him apart was His unwavering commitment to priorities.

Unlike Jesus Christ, many struggle with prioritizing, a challenge that dates back to first humanity's loss of dominion in the Garden of Eden. This loss not only marked the beginning of our struggle with misplaced priorities but also the absence of priorities altogether. Both scenarios bear significant consequences. Without priorities, life becomes a drift, lacking a clear sense of destiny, and often leading to unfulfillment. On the other hand, misplaced priorities result in a life dedicated to the wrong pursuits, despite being intensely focused.

Establishing priorities is about determining what holds the highest value, ranking everything in order of importance, and directing our time, attention, and energy accordingly. It is about putting first things first. Successful individuals excel because they know their purpose of existence and therefore know how to set priorities, enabling them to avoid distractions and focus on what matters most. Success, therefore, hinges on effectively utilizing time, as we are the sum of our time investments.

Every morning, we all receive the same time currency: twenty-four hours. Our life's trajectory depends on how we spend and invest this irreplaceable currency. The quality of our life and the impact we leave on others are directly linked to our time investments. Health, wealth, wisdom, and spiritual maturity are outcomes of intentional time allocation. Time, in essence, shapes who we become and defines our legacy.

Investing time wisely and with purpose is key to preserving and protecting life. Purpose is the foundation of priorities. Without a clear sense of purpose, establishing priorities becomes challenging.

Humanity, in its search for a simple formula for a successful, fulfilling life, often searching for that one key to unlock the door to the right, effective, successful, fulfilled life. However, the revelation often lies in a timeless foundational truth and its inherent principles that have been passed down through various generations, cultures, individuals, and circumstances with unwavering integrity. The record of these timeless foundational truth and its inherent principles can be found in the most important legal document ever given to all humanity, known as the Bible. However, despite its importance, the Bible remains one of the most misunderstood books in human history.

The Bible is most widely misunderstood throughout history. For centuries now, numerous philosophies, religious beliefs, cults, rebelled forces, movements, and organizations have been founded based on this most widely misunderstood book. The Bible places a significant emphasis on the essence of being human because, as a human being, you possess inherent dignity and importance to God, the Creator of all things. This concept predates any religious beliefs or convictions that you may hold. It is important to understand this perspective as it helps address any distortions in our cultural upbringing or conditioning that may have influenced our view of the Bible.

This book, Bible is so strange that anytime you read it takes you back to the beginning of time, and it is also so advanced and not as old as we think, and so we need to study and catch up with its clear concepts because it outclass any book ever written on humanity, and eventually outsmart us too. Individuals who did not had a clear-cut concept of Bible from childhood often superimpose their cultural experiences onto it regardless of whether they were raised under anarchy, fascism, socialism, communism, dictatorship, monarchy, democracy, or any form of government. This grave misconception is further compounded when this particular individual has a religious mind because he or she will read the Bible from a tainted religious perspective" (Excerpts from Chapter 1 of "Where Am I from?"—The Loss Human Factor).

Therefore, it is very imperative to know and importantly understand in exploring the Bible, particularly the book of Genesis, sheds light on God's priorities for our lives. The Bible serves as a guide to understanding the principles of a successful and purposeful life, emphasizing the importance of aligning our priorities with God's priorities.

BEFORE YOU EXISTED...

(Excerpts from Chapter 2 of "Where Am I from?"—The Loss Human Factor)

When a manufacturer sets out to make a product, the very first decision revolves around where they will source the materials from, often referred to as raw materials. This critical choice is the bedrock upon which the entire product rests. It is not just about obtaining the materials; it is about understanding why those specific materials are chosen. This initial step is fundamental and universally followed in the world of manufacturing.

Before embarking on the actual production, manufacturers meticulously map out the raw materials required, aligning them with the purpose and intended functions of the product. This strategic alignment essentially defines the inherent capabilities of the product and ultimately shapes its design. Skipping or neglecting this meticulous process is not an option for any manufacturer worth their salt.

In essence, the design of the product is not just about its appearance; it directly correlates with its inherent capabilities. These capabilities, in turn, dictate its functions, which intricately weave together to serve the purpose for which the product is intended. And interestingly, this purpose-driven aspect often determines the choice of raw materials, closing the loop of this intricate manufacturing process.

This methodical approach to crafting a product is not a recent innovation; it is a principle deeply ingrained in the history of human manufacturing. Even in the realms of evolutionary theories, this natural process stands tall as a cornerstone. It is a sequence of events that has remained sacrosanct, never breached or disregarded throughout humanity's history.

These are the foundational principles we need not to forget:

- The purpose of a product (resource) defines the inherent function (capability) of the product to be made.
- The inherent function (capability) of the product (resource) determines the selection of the nature of the composition of the raw material (source) from which the product is to be made.
- The nature of the composition of the raw material (source) defines the nature of the composition of the product (resource) made.
- Whatever is in the raw material (source) is in the product (resource) made.
- The product (resource) possesses the same nature of the composition of the raw material (source) from which it was made.
- Therefore, whatever the raw material (source) is, the product (resource) made from it is.

When God, the Creator of all things, set out to bring the universe into existence, He harnessed the potency of His spoken Word with great deliberation. It is essential to grasp the careful approach He employed. Whenever God, the Creator of all things, aimed to fashion something, He meticulously determined both the purpose and the nature of what He intended to create. Subsequently, He articulated His intentions to the very components from which He desired the creation to emerge. The crucial point to comprehend is this foundational principle: In God's natural creative process, He initially ascertained the purpose and nature of the desired creation, then specified the raw materials for its construction. His spoken words to these materials brought forth precisely what He had envisioned. Thus, whenever God, the Creator of all things, embarked on the act of creation, He methodically outlined the purpose, nature, and composition of His envisioned creation, ensuring that His spoken words had a direct and precise impact on the materialization of His creative intent.

In the foundational principles found in the first book of the Old Testament, in Genesis chapter 1, verses 11, 14–15, 20–21, and 24, we uncover a crucial aspect of God's creative process. When God, the Creator of all things, intended to bring forth the vast variety of plant life—grasses, herbs, seeds, fruits, trees, flowers, and more—He articulated His Word:

> *"Let the earth [dirt] bring forth vegetation: plants yielding seed and fruit trees bearing fruit in which is their seed, each according to its kind, on the earth"* (Genesis 1:11).

118

This proclamation illustrates God's intention for the entire plant kingdom to emerge from the soil. His spoken Word directed towards the dirt resulted in the manifestation of His command, as the verse states, "And it was so." Consequently, every aspect of the plant kingdom is fundamentally derived from the earth itself; hence, when plants wither and return to the ground, they simply return to their originating or primary substance—dirt.

Likewise, when we partake of fruits like apples, mangoes, tomatoes, or peppers, it is crucial to recognize that we are essentially consuming elements of the earth. Although the truth remains that these are distinct fruits, their essence is rooted in the soil—emphasizing that when left unattended, they decompose back into dirt, reverting to their primary substance as directed by God's natural creative command.

This principle extends further to the creation of celestial bodies. When God desired the existence of the sun, moon, stars, and all luminous bodies—referred to in Hebrew as "māʾôr" translated as "lights"—He spoke,

> *"Let there be lights in the expanse [firmaments] of the heavens to separate the day from the night. And let them be for signs and for seasons, and for days and years; and let them be lights in the expanse [firmaments] of the heavens to give light on the earth" (Genesis 1:14–15).*

In this instance, God's command was directed at the firmaments of the heavens, described in Hebrew as "rāqîaʿ,"

signifying the visible arch of the sky, which is composed of gases. Therefore, the sun, being a product of God's directive to the "firmaments of the heavens," is essentially comprised entirely of gases.

Furthering this understanding, Genesis chapter 1, verses 20–21 detail God's desire for aquatic and aerial life. When God sought to bring forth creatures inhabiting the waters—fishes—and those soaring through the skies—birds—He spoke to the water-dirt, declaring,

> *"Let the waters swarm with swarms of living creatures, and let birds fly above the earth across the expanse [firmaments] of the heavens" (Genesis 1:20–21).*

Hence, the creatures dwelling in water, such as fishes, and those occupying the skies, like birds, are essentially products of the water-dirt and are fundamentally composed of this element. When these creatures cease to live, they return entirely to their source—water-dirt for aquatic creatures and dirt for birds.

Moreover, when God aimed to bring forth the entirety of the animal kingdom, He proclaimed,

> *"Let the earth bring forth living creatures according to their kinds: livestock, creeping things, and beasts of the earth according to their kinds" (Genesis 1:24).*

As a result, every creature from the animal kingdom, upon its demise, returns to being fundamentally comprised of dirt—fulfilling precisely what God spoke into existence.

These principles underscore an essential aspect of the natural creative process—the origin and sustenance of all living entities. Everything that emerges in creation retains an inherent connection to its source (where it came from) for sustenance and existence. Plants, came from the earth, thrive by drawing sustenance from the same soil. Stars, came from the firmaments of the heavens, exist within that realm to sustain their luminosity. Fishes, came from water-dirt, thrive solely in aquatic environments. Similarly, animals, came from dirt, derive their sustenance from various aspects of the earth—be it plants or other natural elements—signifying their intimate link to their source for thriving and continuation of life. Therefore, God is your Father, which is translated from the Greek word "patér," meaning:

- One who has infused his own spirit into others, activating and governing their minds.
- Of all rational and intelligent beings, whether angels or men, because he is their ancestor, preserver, guardian, and protector.
- The author of a family or society of persons animated by the same spirit of himself.
- Progenitor of a people.
- A more remote ancestor, the founder of a family or tribe.
- Generator.
- One advanced in years, a senior.

The word "Father" also in Hebrew is "Aba" or "Abba," meaning source and sustainer. God is your Source because you came out from Him. That is why it is important not to address anyone on this physical planet Earth as your spiritual father because there is only One who is God. Jesus Christ addresses this to us all humanity:

> "And don't address anyone here on earth as 'Father,' for only God in Heaven is your spiritual Father" (Matthew 23:9).

ON YOUR EXISTENCE...

(Excerpts from Chapter 2 of "Where Am I from?"—The Loss Human Factor)

In Genesis chapter 1, verse 26, a notable deviation occurs in God's creative process when He, the Creator of all things, expresses His intent (purpose) to bring forth a distinct species—man. God declares to Himself,

> "Let Us make man in Our image, according to Our likeness; let them have dominion over the fish of the sea, over the birds of the air, and over the cattle, over all the earth and over every creeping thing that creeps on the earth."

This dominion, described in the Bible transliterate the Hebrew word "mam-lakah" or "miśrâ" which is equivalent of the Greek word "basileia," which can also be translated as "Kingdom," "World," "Government," "Sovereignty," "Leadership," "Rulership," "Royalty," "Management," "Master-ship," "Administration," "Authority," or "Influence," signified the responsibility given to humanity. All these ideal terms that define dominion in the Bible are connected.

As I stated earlier in Chapter 3 of this book—an excerpts there: "In effect, God expects His created beings, us, humanity to dominate everything on Earth. Notice that nowhere was it stated that dominion extends over fellow human beings. God never intended for us to dominate ourselves. He specified what we humans were to have dominion over—thus, the creation and the earth. You were not designed to be dominated. That is why when you find yourself being dominated by another human being, there is this innate aspect of your human spirit that will urge you to throw off this unnatural restraint.

The concept of dominion relates to you, which includes ruling, managing, controlling, influencing, leading, governing, mastering, and having authority. This means anything that originates from the earth, whose raw materials come from the earth, is what you are meant to dominate. Your physical body came from the dirt of the earth, but it was not meant to dominate you as a spirit being. You are not your physical body; you are a spirit being, possessing a soul, residing in a physical body. Your spirit, as you were meant to, should dominate your physical body. So, if your physical body is dominating you as a spirit being, compelling you to indulge in drug abuse, theft, arrogance, a false sense of superiority, or promiscuity, do not walk around as if you have received some new revelation of life. You are too smart to be in that state. That is precisely a reversal of what your Creator God expects from you.

You were meant to dominate it, to put it under control. You were born to be addicted to dominating the earth, not addicted to anything of the earth dominating you."

It is important to observe this departure: while God previously spoke to various elements like earth [dirt], firmaments of the heavens, and water-dirt when creating other life forms, the creation of man takes a unique turn as God speaks directly to Himself.

In essence, God draws man out of His own being, indicating that humanity came from God Himself. The term for "man" in its root Hebrew form, "ādām," translates to "spirit beings," underlining the spiritual essence of man. As God is Spirit, He fashioned humanity to share in this spiritual nature. Importantly, spirits inherently lack gender, implying that God, the Creator of all things, transcends gender distinctions. Although masculine expressions are used for clarity, it is vital to recognize the generic representation rather than a specific gender.

The species called "man" is not merely imbued with a spirit; rather, they are spirits themselves, devoid of gender because spirits inherently lack such distinctions. The Bible does not make any reference to male or female spirits, underscoring that humanity, as a species, is defined by being spirit rather than gender-specific. This uniqueness reinforces the importance God places on the entire species of "man."

Genesis 1:27 introduces two distinct natural creative processes employed by God in bringing forth humanity. The terms "create" and "make" are pivotal in understanding these processes. The Hebrew root word for "create" is "bara," signifying bringing something into existence out of nothing, while "make" is derived from the Hebrew "ʿāsâ," meaning bringing something out of existing material. Genesis 1:27 states,

> *"God created man in His own image; in the image of God He created him; male and female He created them."*

This verse emphasizes that, concerning the origin of humanity on Earth, God both created and made man.

In this context, "create" refers to the aspect of man that came out of nothing—directly from the Spirit of God. God, the Creator of all things, spoke the spiritual essence of man into existence. On the other hand, "make" pertains to the physical bodies of man—male and female—formed from the pre-existing material, the dust of the ground or the dirt of the earth. Hence, while the spiritual core of man came from God, the physical bodies came from the earthly elements that God had previously created.

This duality is highlighted in Genesis 2:7:

> *"Then the Lord God formed man from the dust of the ground and breathed into his nostrils the breath or spirit of life, and man became a living being."*

God, in a remarkable act, places the spirit of man into two distinct physical bodies—male and female—both molded from the dust of the ground or the dirt of the earth. The result is a living being, a synthesis of the divine spiritual essence and the earthly physical form. That is the spot where the phrase "living being" shifted to "human being" in a more contemporary way. The word "human" originates from two distinctive words: "humus," indicating earth, dirt, or ground, and "man," signifying spirit beings. So, "human being" essentially refers to a spirit being within a physical body made of earth, dirt, or ground, representing the physical form, whether male or female.

In the inevitable cycle of life and death, our physical bodies, derived from the earth, return to the dirt when we die. Simultaneously, our spirits return to God, the Father of our spirits, completing the interconnected relationship between the divine origin and earthly composition of humanity. God's original design not only emphasizes the significance of the spiritual aspect of humanity but also highlights the harmonious union of the spiritual and the material in the creation of man.

In its effect, God, the Creator of all things, did not bring you out of a salamander, a crocodile, a monkey, an explosive band or any apelike creature or any creature from the waters, as you have heard or learned. You were brought out of God, the Creator of all things Himself.

YOU PRE-EXISTED WITHIN GOD BEFORE YOU EXISTED...

(Excerpts from Chapter 2 of "Where Am I from"—The Loss Human Factor)

THE GREATEST FOUNDATIONAL principle to grasp is that before God assigns a task, He has already instilled in you the capability to accomplish it. He finalizes things in the unseen before initiating them in the seen, echoing God's words through Isaiah:

> *"Remember this, keep it in mind, take it to heart, you rebels. Remember the former things, those of long ago; I AM God, and there is no other; I AM God, and there is none like Me. I make known the end from the beginning, from ancient times, what is still to come. I say, 'My purpose will stand, and I will do all that I please'" (Isaiah 46:10).*

God, the Creator of all things, sets the end before the beginning, ensuring completion before commencement. This process occurred when God designed humanity to dominate the Earth (Genesis 1:26, emphasis added). Essentially, you existed in God before earthly existence. God, a Spirit, spoke to Himself, birthing the species called man, denoting a spirit. He crafted man in a specific way—according to His image and likeness.

Before a manufacturer emblazons their product with an image—icon or logo, they meticulously prepare the product for success. They assemble necessary components, ensuring inherent capacity, and conduct tests. Similarly, God, in bringing you forth, embedded His image and likeness, designing you with inherent abilities. Your future is not external but internal; it is within you. Just as plants bear seeds containing trees, your existence in God holds the blueprint for your purpose, as seen in Genesis 1:11.

God fashioned you from Himself, knowing your capabilities, and placed His image within you. Like a manufacturer confident in their product, God, having tested and equipped you internally, urges you to live up to His design—image and likeness. Your future is not distant; it is within, waiting to unfold. Just as the land produced vegetation with seeds and trees with fruit, God released you onto Earth to dominate for Him.

In its effect, God's preeminent principle involves shaping your internal capacity before external manifestation. You are a deliberate creation, intentionally designed to fulfill your purpose. Just as a manufacturer certifies their product's capabilities before showcasing it, God has certified your potential, daring you to live out the purpose embedded within you. Your existence is not a random occurrence; it is a strategic placement by God, who set the trajectory of your life before its inception.

King David, in the book of Psalms, expressed gratitude to God, the Creator of all things, for the intricacy of human creation, stating,

> *"You made all the delicate, inner parts of my body and knit me together in my mother's womb. I will praise You, for I am fearfully and wonderfully made;*

Marvelous are Your works, and that my soul knows very well" (Psalm 139:13–14).

David's words convey his thankfulness to God, the Creator of all things, acknowledging, "Thank you for making me, for I am made with awe-inspiring care." David is highlighting that God designed humans with a sense of reverence and extraordinary craftsmanship.

The term "fearfully" in this context stems from the Hebrew word "yārē," signifying "to instill fear", "to inspire wonder", "to command respect or divine reverence." Essentially, when God fashioned individuals, He did so with care. It mirrors an artist's meticulousness, driven by the desire to avoid errors. God, in shaping each person, was committed to precision and excellence, thereby inspiring David to exclaim gratitude.

David's praise is rooted in the notion that God's craftsmanship was not merely about creating, but about crafting individuals uniquely. Whether it is the size of one's features - head, eyes, nose, mouth, cheekbones - or the stature and placement of limbs, each detail is purposeful and essential. The formation and arrangement of these physical attributes are intentionally linked to the purpose each individual is destined to fulfill. God's intent was not simply to create, but to intentionally design individuals, ensuring that they are precisely who they are meant to be.

Every aspect of one's physical appearance was deliberately fashioned; the placement of arms and ears, the intricacies of appearance, were all part of God's deliberate design. His meticulous care in shaping individuals was not to make them conform to an arbitrary standard but to ensure they are uniquely suited for their purpose. This attention to detail and care signifies that God did not rush but invested ample time, driven by a profound sense of reverence and desire for perfection.

Isaiah conveyed a profound message in his words:

> *"But now, O LORD, You are our Father; We are the clay, and You our potter; And all we are the work of Your hand... You turn things upside down! Shall the potter be considered of no more account than the clay? Shall the thing that is made say of its maker, He did not make me; or the thing that is formed say of him who formed it, He has no understanding?" (Isaiah 64:8; 29:16).*

Isaiah highlighted the significance of God as the Creator of all things and humanity as the creation. He challenged the notion of questioning the Maker (God the Creator of all things) about the nature of His creation. Isaiah's message was clear: it is a mistake to question why God made you the way you are, because He possesses insights about you that you might not comprehend.

When God fashioned each person, He began by intentionally designing their innermost being, assembling them in the womb. This signifies a meticulous planning by God, choosing precisely where each individual would begin life. Whether someone's physical appearance is black, yellow, white, or any other complexion, it is intentional. God uniquely crafted individuals in the physical form they were meant to be.

The diversity of humanity reflects God's deliberate intention to create a varied and rich tapestry of individuals. God always create a distinct and unique human being, tailored for a specific purpose. Each person is designed intentionally, signifying God's attention to detail and care during the natural creative process.

David's use of the term "wonderfully made" signifies a complexity that English struggles to encapsulate from the original Hebrew word "pālâ." It implies that when God designed and assembled individuals, He did so with a sense of awe and wonder, creating each person as a remarkable, marked-out, distinct, and unique being. This uniqueness often leads others to wonder about an individual's character, potential, and abilities, sometimes resulting in doubt or misunderstandings.

Individuals are meant to stand out, to be extraordinary, and to evoke a sense of marvel in others. They are not supposed to hide behind someone else's personality or be a mere copy of another. Each person is extraordinary in their own right, and comparing oneself to others negates the uniqueness inherent in every individual.

David's affirmation that "my soul knows very well" underlines the importance of self-awareness and self-acceptance. It suggests that seeking affirmation or validation from external sources is not necessary because one's inner self holds the ultimate understanding of their uniqueness and purpose. Relying on external validation may limit one's growth or self-realisation, as others might not fully comprehend or enhance an individual beyond their own understanding.

It is important to embrace where one comes from. You came from God, the Creator of all things, Himself. And to understand that uniqueness and distinctiveness are fundamental aspects of humanity identity. Refusing to be true to oneself, seeking validation from others, or attempting to conform to someone else's standard can hinder personal growth and authenticity.

Upon completing the creating and making of individuals, God, the Creator of all things, does not just stop there. He subjects them to tests to ascertain if they are suited for their designated functions on Earth, to exercise dominion, just as David mentioned: *"For You, O God, have tested [proved] us; You have tried us as silver is tried, refined, and purified" (Psalm 66:10).* This process of testing is likened to refining silver in a crucible.

Similar to how every manufacturer embeds their image—logo or icon on a product, indicating that everything essential for the product's intended function is integrated, God marks individuals with His image. This divine imprint signifies that all necessary elements to fulfill one's purpose have been instilled within. Consequently, nothing needs to be added or removed from the individual.

For a manufacturer, the worst-case scenario is when their product fails to fulfill its purpose, risking damage to the manufacturer's reputation and business. The success of a product is of utmost importance to its maker. Manuals from manufacturers often assert that if the product fails, it should be returned for repair or replacement, all at the manufacturer's expense. This commitment to rectifying issues with the product underscores the significance of its success to the manufacturer.

Likewise, your success holds significance for God. His creations—seeds to grow trees, fishes to swim, birds to fly—exist with specific purposes. If they fail to fulfill these purposes, it tarnishes God's reputation. Therefore, God tests the multitude of individuals on Earth because He desires success for each of them in their respective lives.

The underlying principle is that God's reputation is intertwined with the success of His creations. Just as a manufacturer stands by their product, ensuring it fulfills its intended function, God is invested in His creations, nurturing and supporting them to accomplish their designed purposes.

The testing process individuals undergo is not about creating obstacles or causing harm; rather, it is a means for God to ensure that each person is equipped and capable of fulfilling their unique functions in the world. His desire is for everyone to thrive and succeed in life.

GOD'S PRIORITIES FOR RE-DISCOVERING THE PURPOSE FOR YOUR LIFE

Understanding God's priorities for re-discovering the purpose for our lives is the utmost importance among all priorities in our lives. This provides us with a comprehensive view of the "why" behind our existence on this planet. Let us crawl up into God's thoughts now to discern His priorities for our lives, which He intends us to prioritize as well.

- **Image—Character.**

As stated in Genesis 1:26, *"Let Us make man in Our image,..."* The word "image" from its original word "ṣelem" and it does not mean physical appearance. It literally means you were made in God's *characteristic nature, personality, moral character, and His essential specifications.* All these are classified as one—*image.* So if you want to specifically know what your identity is, you have to look at the Source—God the Creator of all things, because you possessed one hundred percent of His characteristic nature, moral character, personality and essential specifications. Apart from man there is no other specie in existence in Heaven or on this planet Earth, that has God's image, not even angels. We are the only specie that God gave His image to.

Discussing the image that God has given to all humanity requires us to delve into the concept of "moral character." To fulfill your purpose on Earth and make the most of your life, it is crucial to acknowledge that you possess God's moral character. What does this mean? Essentially, it emphasizes the importance of being consistently authentic. Instead of trying to mimic others or create a false image, you should be true to yourself at all times.

Being authentic involves understanding that there is no such thing as a secret life. Actions done in secret, with the belief that no one will find out, have a way of surfacing publicly. Life has its mechanisms for bringing hidden deeds into the open, so thinking you can outsmart life is a fallacy. Furthermore, it is essential to internalize the idea that your destiny is closely linked to your character.

While skills, talents, and gifts can make you exceptional in a particular area, a defective character can undermine everything. Trust from others is directly connected to your character. No matter how skilled or talented you are, humility and the right attitude are crucial. The extent of your success in life hinges on the strength of your character.

People with strong characters have a conviction that they would not compromise their principles for momentary pleasures. Their discipline and focus on goals make them resilient against distractions. Character involves having the determination to stay true to oneself even when faced with challenges. Despite promising futures, individuals lacking a strong character may find themselves in troubled waters.

A person's future success or failure becomes predictable based on their character. Those with flawed characters are unpredictable, lacking principles to guide them. They easily get sidetracked by various pleasures such as alcohol, drugs, promiscuity, and more. In contrast, individuals with character exhibit discipline and are challenging to divert from their chosen path.

God encourages individuals to prioritize His moral character for their lives. People with character are trustworthy and accountable, maintaining consistency between their public and private lives. They do not rely on external instructions but live by their principles, earning the trust of those around them.

The power of one's character should not be underestimated. A defective character can distort one's purpose to the extent of committing grave atrocities, as seen in historical figures like Adolf Hitler. This serves as a stark reminder that a compromised character can lead to destructive outcomes.

In effect, recognizing and embodying God's moral character is essential for leading a purposeful life. Being authentic, maintaining trust through humility, and staying disciplined contribute to a strong character. Your character determines the trajectory of your future, making it a cornerstone for success and a shield against potential pitfalls that could derail you from becoming who you were intended to be as purpose by God, the Creator of all things.

- **Likeness—Faith.**

Your top priority in life is to operate in the way God designed you, and that is exactly God's priority for your life, as stated in Genesis 1:26: *"Let Us make man in Our image, according to Our likeness;..."* This design is centered on faith, a belief inherent in all humanity, not something for religious minds and not for secular minds. Faith is the conviction that your existence has purpose and meaning, empowering you to pursue your goals with confidence, knowing that God supports you. Without faith, life loses its essential driving force, akin to an automobile running out of gasoline.

A life devoid of faith in God is more susceptible to succumbing to suicide, especially when faced with seemingly endless challenges. In such situations, fear emerges as the mind's presumption of non-existent realities, with its ultimate aim being to erode our faith in God. Fear, a self-constructed and self-nurtured emotion, takes hold when faith wanes, pushing individuals towards the brink of despair.

The absence of faith can lead to a sense of hopelessness, and this is why maintaining faith is crucial. Faith acknowledges that life is a mystery, filled with aspects beyond our comprehension, control, and explanation. Living in the present becomes possible through faith, as it recognizes that the certainty of life lies in the immediate moments.

Those who navigate life with faith find themselves equipped to handle disappointments, understanding that faith encapsulates the mysterious nature of life. Faith prompts proactive and self-determined actions, allowing individuals to take the initiative rather than passively waiting. In essence, faith is more than intellectual agreement; it is about practicality and actively engaging with life.

Planning, the greatest act of faith, is emphasized as a means to translate God's vision for your life into reality. Taking control of your life through planning involves bringing God's purpose into tangible existence, bridging the gap between vision and reality. It underscores the importance of relying on faith in

God rather than material possessions, as things can be lost, but God remains a constant and permanent presence.

Living effectively, maximizing your potential, and fulfilling God's purpose for your life hinge on holding onto your faith. Faith becomes the guiding force that propels you forward, ensuring that you navigate life's complexities with confidence and purpose.

- **Presence—Environment.**

Every living thing has a purpose that requires the right environment. Birds, made to fly, find fulfilment in the open sky. If you cage a bird, it cannot fulfill its purpose – its environment limits its fulfilment. Fish, created to swim, find fulfilment in water; swimming is their natural state. Taking a fish out of water causes immediate problems. Similarly, before creating life, God prepared suitable environments, like oceans and fertile land. For humanity, a moderate climate and food were not enough. Adam and Eve needed a place surrounded by God's presence – Garden of Eden, as mentioned in the Bible:

> *"The LORD God took the man [male and female] and put him in the Garden of Eden..." (Genesis 2:15).*

This environment "where God positioned us is referred to in the Bible as the 'Garden of Eden.' The terms 'Garden' and 'Eden' originate from Hebrew concepts and carry somewhat unconventional meanings that may not readily align with human intellect when translated into the English language.

This is largely due to the fact that English, while widespread, can sometimes be limiting in its expressive capacity.

The term 'Garden' derives from a Hebrew word denoting 'order', 'enclosure', or 'a fenced-in area.' Similarly, 'Eden' offers intriguing interpretations, signifying a 'delightful spot', a 'moment', the 'presence' of God, an 'opened gate', or an 'access point.' In simpler terms, 'Eden' symbolizes a delightful earthly location where God's presence is accessible, serving as an open gateway to Heaven. In essence, the Garden of Eden signifies that everything present in Heaven was manifested in that specific earthly location. It is of paramount importance to grasp that God, the Creator of all things, did not commence the human race on planet Earth by dispersing individuals across the entire surface or letting them randomly stumble upon His essence. Instead, God deliberately placed humanity in a particular orderly and delightful location known as the Garden of Eden" (Excerpts from Chapter 9 of "Where Am I from?"—The Loss Human Factor).

God's priority for you is to be in His presence, as that is where you can re-discover and fulfill your purpose. While you may build numerous relationships, true fulfillment only comes when God is at the center. The key is being in an environment where you can consistently connect with God and embrace your authentic self. If an environment does not introduce you to yourself but instead pushes you to conform to others, it is not the right environment for you.

In times when you find yourself in an unsuitable environment, choosing loneliness becomes necessary. This happens because those around you may expect you to conform to their ways, diverting you from your unique path. Re-discovering your uniqueness, realizing your importance, and understanding your purpose may lead to a period of loneliness, but this loneliness is important for personal growth.

History shows that many influential figures found themselves during times of loneliness. Examples include Moses in the wilderness, Jesus Christ in the desert, and Paul of Tarsus on the road to Damascus. They willingly embraced loneliness, focusing on their visions despite the isolation. What made them compelling was not their loneliness, but their determination to pursue their calling or fulfill their purpose. Utilizing loneliness effectively drew people towards them, transforming their loneliness into meaningful connections.

To truly be yourself when surrounded by an unsupportive environment, choosing loneliness is a deliberate decision. If you are constantly surrounded by everyone in the world, you risk losing yourself in the crowd. The question becomes whether you are willing to prioritize God's priority for you, taking on the responsibility of becoming the person you were meant to be.

- **Work—Becoming.**

Humanity was once consumed with living life, with no time to make a living. This changed when they rebelled against God, leading to their fall from dominion, as outlined in Genesis 3:17. God's original intention for humans was not merely to secure a livelihood but to make a positive impact. However, our rebellion altered this dynamic, and to this day, humans are unique in being creatures created by God who seek employment but often fail to utilize their abilities effectively.

Modern education tends to prepare individuals for employment rather than empowering them for deployment. Unlike seeds growing into trees, fish swimming, or birds flying, humans have confined themselves to a reliance on jobs without fully engaging in work. This has resulted in a curse, where individuals secure jobs but fail to work—contribute meaningfully. While a job presents an opportunity to work, many individuals fall short of realizing their full potential.

The paradox lies in the fact that the prevailing fear in today's world is the fear of job loss. Jobs are not primarily meant for making a living; instead, they are avenues for individuals to express their capabilities and contribute meaningfully. Genesis 2:15 illustrates that God placed humans in the Garden of Eden to work, with the Greek word "eregon" emphasizing that work is a process of becoming oneself.

Work is a transformative journey. It involves leveraging one's talents, gifts and skills to improve the status quo and find fulfillment. It is a departure from a survival-driven mindset that focuses solely on necessities like food, clothing, and shelter. The danger arises when jobs become disconnected from work, leading to a life devoid of purpose.

The core message of this book revolves around the concept of becoming oneself. In the subsequent chapters we will delve into this concept, exploring it in a broader context. The key takeaway is that work should not merely be a means of making a living; it should be a source of fulfillment, enabling individuals to be true to themselves and make valuable contributions to the world around them, that is exactly the priority of God for humanity to which He intends us to make it as our priority too.

- **"Take care of it"—Improve.**

God's priority for humanity is evident in Genesis 2:15, where it says, *"The LORD God took the man and put him in the Garden of Eden to work it and take care of it."* To "take care of it" means to improve, and improvement involves bringing out the best in everything. This reflects God's priority for your life—to enhance the quality of every life around you, including your own. God wants you to positively influence, bring out, and draw out the best in the people around you. Instead of trying to make others like you, God desires you to assist them in becoming their true selves as you grow into your own identity.

God, as the Creator of all things, does not promote a "be more like me" mentality. He does not want you to impose your identity on others, thinking that everyone should follow the same path as you. Comparing yourself to others who may not understand themselves leads to deception, pushing them onto a path that may not be right for them. God encourages you to help others re-discover their own paths rather than molding them into replicas of yourself. What works for you may not be suitable for someone else.

If your journey towards becoming yourself is not positively impacting the lives of those around you and bringing out the best in them, but instead, suppressing their unique selves to make them conform to yourself, you are wasting their potential. God's priority is for you to uplift others, helping them find their selves. It is not about making everyone like you; it is about contributing to the significance of their lives.

In embracing God's priority for your life, recognize that your journey is unique and tailored for you. Avoid the pitfall of thinking that what worked for you will work for everyone else. Instead, assist others in uncovering their own paths, understanding that what may seem right for you could be detrimental to someone else. By doing so, you align with God's priority for your life and make it a priority to bring out the best in those around you.

In effect, make it your priority to uplift, encourage, and empower others to become the best versions of themselves, just as God intended for you.

- *His Word*—Idea.

God, the Creator of all things, began communicating His intentions to humanity in the Garden of Eden, as described in Genesis 2:16-17, and continues to do so to this day. As we have learned, the purpose of a thing resides in the mind of the creator of the thing, so as the purpose of our lives can be found in the mind of the Creator of our lives, this, God. To grasp this purpose, we must seek God and delve into His thoughts. Remarkably, God translates His purpose for our existence from

His mind to ours, presenting it as an idea for us to comprehend. Contrary to popular belief, God communicates with us through a straightforward transmission of ideas, rather than cryptic messages.

Each person shares a common thread: the presence of ideas. These ideas, akin to seeds, are planted by God in our minds and, when nurtured, blossom into powerful imaginations surpassing mere knowledge. When these imaginative seeds are cultivated further, they develop into action plans, eventually shaping our reality. God consistently communicates with us by implanting ideas into our minds—a process often overlooked. Remarkably, God instills ideas even in minds unaccustomed to great thinking.

As long as you live, God will always impart ideas into your thinking womb. And when God imparts ideas into your thinking womb, they never fade away. This means they will persist, causing frustration, discomfort, and keeping you awake until you create an action plan to turn them into reality. These ideas will consistently reveal your potential, not a measure of your intelligence quotient (IQ) test. Moreover, they will always surpass the capacity of your thinking womb, making you feel inexperienced, like a novice or virgin before God. This is because you have not executed such ideas before, and you lack the experience and knowledge of the process to bring them into reality. Hence, you must follow God with a measure of fear, as the ideas He imparts demand that you seek His guidance for the necessary steps.

Friend, always remember too that God's ideas surpass the limitations of your mobile money wallet, your cash in the bank account, or any savings and resources you possess. God intentionally challenges you in these areas to emphasize that these ideas originate from Him.

It is necessary to recognize that God's ideas align with His Word and are consistent, tailored for different seasons of our lives. These ideas serve as a guiding light, unveiling your purpose through visionary images in the eyes of your mind. If you cannot visualize your life's purpose, you may not be attuned to God's communication.

Accessing God's communication is not through religious affiliations but by returning to His presence, which can be found in your room, bathroom, kitchen, car, or any secluded space. Escaping the noise of the crowd, breaking away from the flow of life, and engaging in prayer, worship, and praise re-creates an environment where you can truly hear from God and re-discover your destined self. Referring to God's Word as an "idea carrier" emphasizes its function in conveying ideas that demand your unwavering attention, making them a priority. These ideas are not about religious rituals; instead, they guide you towards the person you were meant to become.

Chapter 5: Principles To Think About Before You Take Your Last Breath

———

1. Becoming yourself is a monumental achievement in a world constantly pushing you to conform. Trusting yourself is key—do not yield to societal pressures that conflict with what you sees in the eyes of your mind—vision. Do not carry guilt for not meeting others' expectations; focus on fulfilling your unique life purpose. You are not here to follow religious or school paths forced upon you by others; embrace your authenticity.

2. The real battles are not for breaking Guinea World Records; it is breaking free from world's expectations. Living according to the world's expectations makes us lose ourselves, pleasing others at the expense of authenticity. People offer condolences in death but disrupt your peace while alive, only to pray for your rest in peace after you are gone. Ironically, I congratulate the dead; they remain true to themselves.

3. When God paints a picture in your mind, do not dismiss it; it holds power to change your life. Do not hold back due to fear; your best work comes after embracing your worst attempts.

4. Every morning, we all receive the same time currency: twenty-four hours. Our life's trajectory depends on

how we spend and invest this irreplaceable currency. The quality of our life and the impact we leave on others are directly linked to our time investments. Health, wealth, wisdom, and spiritual maturity are outcomes of intentional time allocation. Time, in essence, shapes who we become and defines our legacy.

5. Your physical body came from the dirt of the earth, but it was not meant to dominate you as a spirit being. You are not your physical body; you are a spirit being, possessing a soul, residing in a physical body. Your spirit, as you were meant to, should dominate your physical body. So, if your physical body is dominating you as a spirit being, compelling you to indulge in drug abuse, theft, arrogance, a false sense of superiority, or promiscuity, do not walk around as if you have received some new revelation of life. You are too smart to be in that state. That is precisely a reversal of what your Creator God expects from you.

6. The greatest foundational principle to grasp is that before God assigns a task, He has already instilled in you the capability to accomplish it. He finalizes things in the unseen before initiating them in the seen.

7. God fashioned you from Himself, knowing your capabilities, and placed His image within you. Like a manufacturer confident in their product, God, having tested and equipped you internally, urges you to live up to His design—image and likeness. Your future is not distant; it is within, waiting to unfold. Just as the land produced vegetation with seeds and trees with

fruit, God released you onto Earth to dominate for Him.

8. You are a deliberate creation, intentionally designed to fulfill your purpose. Just as a manufacturer certifies their product's capabilities before showcasing it, God has certified your potential, daring you to live out the purpose embedded within you. Your existence is not a random occurrence; it is a strategic placement by God, who set the trajectory of your life before its inception.

9. Being authentic involves understanding that there is no such thing as a secret life. Actions done in secret, with the belief that no one will find out, have a way of surfacing publicly. Life has its mechanisms for bringing hidden deeds into the open, so thinking you can outsmart life is a fallacy.

10. Trust from others is directly connected to your character. No matter how skilled or talented you are, humility and the right attitude are crucial. The extent of your success in life hinges on the strength of your character.

11. The absence of faith can lead to a sense of hopelessness, and this is why maintaining faith is crucial. Faith acknowledges that life is a mystery, filled with aspects beyond our comprehension, control, and explanation. Living in the present becomes possible through faith, as it recognizes that the certainty of life lies in the immediate moments.

12. God's priority for you is to be in His presence, as that is where you can re-discover and fulfill your purpose.

While you may build numerous relationships, true fulfillment only comes when God is at the center. The key is being in an environment where you can consistently connect with God and embrace your authentic self. If an environment does not introduce you to yourself but instead pushes you to conform to others, it is not the right environment for you.

13. To truly be yourself when surrounded by an unsupportive environment, choosing loneliness is a deliberate decision. If you are constantly surrounded by everyone in the world, you risk losing yourself in the crowd.

14. God's original intention for humans was not merely to secure a livelihood but to make a positive impact. However, our rebellion altered this dynamic, and to this day, humans are unique in being creatures created by God who seek employment but often fail to utilize their abilities effectively.

15. Modern education tends to prepare individuals for employment rather than empowering them for deployment.

16. God, as the Creator of all things, does not promote a "be more like me" mentality. He does not want you to impose your identity on others, thinking that everyone should follow the same path as you. Comparing yourself to others who may not understand themselves leads to deception, pushing them onto a path that may not be right for them. God encourages you to help others re-discover their own paths rather than molding them into replicas of

yourself. What works for you may not be suitable for someone else.

17. Each person shares a common thread: the presence of ideas. These ideas, akin to seeds, are planted by God in our minds and, when nurtured, blossom into powerful imaginations surpassing mere knowledge. When these imaginative seeds are cultivated further, they develop into action plans, eventually shaping our reality. God consistently communicates with us by implanting ideas into our minds—a process often overlooked. Remarkably, God instills ideas even in minds unaccustomed to great thinking.

18. As long as you live, God will always impart ideas into your thinking womb. And when God imparts ideas into your thinking womb, they never fade away. This means they will persist, causing frustration, discomfort, and keeping you awake until you create an action plan to turn them into reality. These ideas will consistently reveal your potential, not a measure of your intelligence quotient (IQ) test. Moreover, they will always surpass the capacity of your thinking womb, making you feel inexperienced, like a novice or virgin before God. This is because you have not executed such ideas before, and you lack the experience and knowledge of the process to bring them into reality. Hence, you must follow God with a measure of fear, as the ideas He imparts demand that you seek His guidance for the necessary steps.

CHAPTER

6

Becoming Yourself

———

Nothing always strikes me as how we cherish ourselves more than others, yet we value their opinions about us more than our own. Start afresh by assessing each person's opinion based on who they are, not who you are. Be convinced living as if this is your second chance, detached from the expectations of humanity. Embrace your new life as if you were already dead to societal expectations.

Live with the mindset of a dying person who is on borrowed time, liberate yourself from the grip of others' opinions, and do not delay anything that brings you fulfillment. Polish the details of your life daily, recognizing that each day's experiences are distinct from your life's essence. Consider what you do with these experiences, rather than letting them define your existence.

Trust in yourself; perceive every occurrence as a divine progression, steering you towards a necessary path, even if it seems like an obstacle. Have faith that it is God's way of propelling you toward the life He intended for you. Live that purpose, and success and unexpected greatness will unfold in your everyday moments.

As we, all humanity, are in the race between ourselves and our graveyards, encompassing the broad spectrum of lives that have once existed on the surface of this planet, those living presently, and those yet to come, I have found no clearer or more concise definition of purpose, both theoretically and pragmatically, than the one encapsulated below, which resonates within the human spirit of the average person. Here it is:

Purpose is the conviction of a vision that is created by inspiration, which becomes a passion for living.

In the subsequent pages of this chapter, we are going to elaborate more on the key terminologies in the definition of purpose, to which I am deeply convinced in my spirit that it will change both your inner and outer outlook on life.

THE INHERENT ELEMENTS OF PURPOSE

I am absolutely certain within myself that understanding the purpose of life from the perspective intended by God, the Creator of all things, may encompass certain foundational elements: conviction, vision, aspiration, passion, and possibly more. To ascertain whether one has re-discovered the purpose of their life bestowed by God, it will consistently include these elements. It is important to note that these elements are inherent, meaning they are not something that can be decided upon or removed by a group of people sitting around a table. Beneath the surface of what defines the purpose of human existence lies these inherent elements. I invite you to carefully read through them with focused attention, observing yourself and perhaps those around you without passing judgment. Let us explore these inherent elements of what God's purpose for our lives involves in greater depth:

- **Conviction.**

In the Greek concept, conviction implies being strongly convinced or persuaded of something. In the Latin concept, it denotes proving or demonstrating the truth or correctness of something, often in legal proceedings where evidence is used to establish beliefs. Additionally, in the Hebrew concept, conviction conveys the idea of "to live" or "to be alive," suggesting a strong and living belief or faith in something.

If we meticulously synthesize these various interpretations based on the aforementioned concepts, it would refer to a sense of significance in one's philosophy or belief system that produces a conceptually convincing and compelling view, persistently persuading one to act, demonstrate, or live by it. The emphasis lies on a conceptually convincing and compelling view, where conviction goes beyond mere intellectual knowledge; it becomes a certainty that one has something essential to live for. It entails a wholehearted commitment to a belief system that is stronger than any belief system that may derail you. Consequently, these convictions serve as guiding principles for one's life, infusing it with significance. They provide the moral and ethical compass by which individuals navigate their actions and decisions. Your convictions are instrumental in shaping your character, molding you into a person dedicated to a set of standards, unwavering in the face of challenges or temptations. In essence, having convictions is the cornerstone of personal stability and trustworthiness.

In the midst of life's temptations, convictions act as a steadfast anchor, preventing one from being swayed by the winds of circumstance. When everything else seems uncertain, your convictions remain a constant, providing you with the strength and determination to stay true to your principles.

Your convictions are not mere abstract concepts; they are the lifeblood of your belief system. They define who you are, what you stand for, and how you engage with the world. They are the moral fiber that holds together the fabric of your character.

Your conviction is a belief in yourself. Your entire life is controlled and determined by your belief system about yourself. It is impossible to separate your life from your belief system. Your conviction is what bounces you forward even when you want to go back; it is a willingness and capacity to walk alone even when the entire world is against you. Your conviction is a certainty that you are unique and necessary to the world.

Also, your conviction is a deep seated belief that, you are not a copy of anyone else. It is genuine confidence based on your natural ability, a sense of inherent significant, and the knowledge that there is something you need to do without external urging. No one else can do what makes your existence necessary. This conviction quells fear, instills a confidence not commonly found, and may appear to come from somewhere else in the eyes of many. This conviction is often mistaken for arrogance by the insecure. It revolves around your belief about yourself, a belief that you have rediscovered what you need to do, always vivid in the eyes of your mind.

- **Vision.**

Your cherished conviction transforms into a vivid vision in the eyes of your mind, or subconscious mind, or heart, not merely a visual perception. This vision is exclusive to you; only you are intended to see it. Even if those around you or the world fail to see what you envision, do not abandon it. Every vision has its first believer, and that is the individual who has faith in it.

Unlike what society often suggests, a vision is distinct from ambition or mission. It offers a photograph of your future, not a self-centered desire or personal ambition. Your vision influences how you allocate your time, determines your priorities, guides your energy towards various pursuits, dictates your financial decisions, influences your attire, shapes your attitude towards life, and even impacts your dietary choices.

Your vision transcends mere interests and sensory pleasures, residing in the depths of your desires. It persists despite challenges and temptations, unselfish and deeply rooted in the belief that it alone can bring you fulfillment.

The vision you see in your mind's eye liberates you from the limitations of what your physical eyes perceive, allowing you to embrace the possibilities sensed by your heart. It empowers you to navigate the unseen and unknown aspects of life, making suffering and disappointment more manageable or bearable. Your vision is the unwavering faith that amidst uncertainty, troubles, heartaches, tribulations, mistakes, and losses, everything will fall into place, resulting in joy and amazement. Your vision forcibly lifts you from depression, propels you beyond discouragement, and erases the concept of impossibility from your mind. Without vision, humanity would be mired in disillusionment and confusion.

Your vision extends beyond what your eyes can see, providing a reason for you to live. Your vision endure even beyond death; if it fades with you, it was not a vision but mere ambition. Vision is a powerful force that compels you to translate it into reality, causing frustration and discomfort until it materializes. Every vision instills discipline, fostering self-development and service to humanity including everything in your environment. Vision uplifts moral standards and preserves human values and dignity. Your vision can never makes you insensitive to others; instead, it contributes to the well-being of humanity, upholding moral principles and safeguarding lives.

- **Inspiration.**

Vision is created by "inspiration," a concept originating from the Greek term meaning "divine deposit" or "god-breath." This means the source of your vision does not come from your culture or society; it comes from God, who gives a purpose that provides a conceptual view of the purpose you were born to fulfill. In other words, purpose is an assignment with a divine touch.

Vision is not something that can be created or invented by you, society, or the world. What we often invent to align ourselves with and call our vision is normally called "ambition." Ambition is invented by you based on societal expectations about who you should be, what you should accomplish, and the path you should take. Our society or the world gives us "ambition" and not "vision"; they always want us to conform to what I considered a mediocre life.

Through this, they stifle and strike down our vision, instilling a deep fear in us not to believe what we see in the eyes of our minds. They tell us, "Look, it's not true, what you are seeing doesn't exist because we cannot see it. If it truly exists, we would see it too by now, so you shouldn't bother yourself with it because it's just an abstract, a result of your intellectual agreement. It hasn't been done before, and it doesn't align with the normalcy of our culture and the global world."

They may even try to measure your experiences and knowledge about it with theirs, telling you "lack of knowledge, my people perish." In other words, they tell you that your experiences and knowledge do not match with what you want to accomplish, and besides, they are wiser on that than you. But always remember that their billions of sophisticated intellectual reasons about your vision do not make it invalid; neither did it come from them. Your vision was generated by God. This is what God says about you: *"Remember the former things, those of long ago; I am God, and there is no other; I am God, and there is none like me. I make known the end from the beginning, from ancient times, what is still to come. I say: My purpose will stand, and I will do all that I please" (Isaiah 46:9-10).*

Notice what God said: *"I make known the end from the beginning, from ancient times, what is still to come" (verse 10).* In other words, God was saying He does not only set your end before He made your beginning on Earth necessary, but also He makes your end known to you in the eyes of your mind at your beginning. That is exactly what inspiration means; it means "divine deposit" or "god-breath." That means it is God, the Creator of all things, Himself that has deposited or breathed that into you, making you see the photograph of your end.

In the book of Ecclesiastes, there is profound wisdom King Solomon encapsulated there. It says: *"I have seen the God-given task (purpose) with which the sons of men are to be occupied. He has made everything beautiful in its time. He has also set eternity in the hearts of men; yet they cannot fathom what God has done from beginning to end" (Ecclesiastes 3:10-11).* In simple terms, King Solomon was saying that we cannot do away with this vision God has inherently instilled in us because if we try, it will frustrate, hurt, make us uncomfortable, and that is inherently natural to feel that until we release that vision out of ourselves.

The burden he is talking about is then described using the word "beautiful," meaning mature. It is meant to be worked out into reality not by miracle or magic but with our potentials. He continues and says, *"He has also set eternity in the hearts of men,"* which is something we do not even know how it is going to become a reality to live. But God promises us something in the book of Proverbs, Isaiah, Ephesians, and Jeremiah. He said, *"Many are the plans in a man's heart, but it is the LORD's purpose that prevails" (Proverbs 19:21). "...My purpose will stand, and I will do all that I please" (Isaiah 46:10). "For I know the thoughts that I think toward you, says the LORD, thoughts of peace and not of evil, to give you a future and a hope" (Jeremiah 29:11). "In Him, we were also chosen, having been predestined according to the plan of Him who works out everything in conformity with the purpose of His will" (Ephesians 1:11).*

From the four scriptures, God is saying that your plans are okay as you decide what to do with your life on this planet and the purpose you have given your life. However, His purpose is more important and powerful because it will prevail over yours and will be accomplished no matter what. He also said that between your beginning and your end is called a plan. Your plans are okay, but in case they do not align with His purpose for your life, He will work out that plan to conform with His purpose for your life, which is good and not evil but always propels you forward towards what you see in the eyes of your mind.

Psalm 57:2 and Psalm 138:8 say not only did God make your existence necessary for a purpose, but He will fulfill His purpose for your life. That is amazing. So, friend, never overlook what you see in the eyes of your mind; it was given to you only by God, the Creator of all things. So do not panic, do not run away from it, and do not say that because the people who hold dear to your heart and have great anointing or resources can not see what you see, that vision is invalid. God's vision He has deposited in you never lies to you as you see it in the eyes of your mind: *"For the vision is yet for an appointed time and it hastens to the end [fulfillment]; it will not deceive or disappoint. Though it tarry, wait earnestly for it, because it will surely come; it will not be behindhand on its appointed day"* (Habakkuk 2:3). It will not happen on your timetable but on God's timetable because that is the right timetable, and you need to go by that because you will never miss any opportunity of greatness that divinity will expose you to. God is the only giver of vision, not you or any humanity.

- **Passion.**

Passion is a profound, compelling desire that drives an individual to be devoted to living by specific principles, all geared towards fulfilling their purpose. This intense desire not only guides and motivates the person but propels them beyond mere interest or temporary pleasures. It empowers them to defy challenges such as opposition, adversity, failure, disappointment, and discouragement, confiding them into a prison of deep personal commitment. This commitment extends beyond merely living for a vision; it involves a willingness to die for it that aims to benefit humanity as a whole.

Passion represents a powerful sense of personal obligation, determination, and a readiness to sacrifice personal ambitions, comfort, and life's pleasures to turn a vision into reality for the greater good. Individuals living with passion find themselves prisoners of their visions, risking their lives to fulfill them. Their resilience stands firm even when faced with unexpected and repeated storms of life, including failed examinations, painful breakups, emotional trauma, life imprisonment, serious health issues, setbacks, mistakes, job loss, loss of position, and more.

These passionate individuals are not passive observers waiting for everything to be easy before taking action. They are initiators, driven by a deep inner compulsion to become what they were destined to be. Society often struggles to understand such individuals, labeling them as "demons," "too know," "show-offs," "busy for nothing," or even "stupid." This is because they are not merely interested in certain pursuits; they are committed to achieving what they were born to become, establishing principles to live by and staying true to their course.

Passionate individuals are willing to invest their entire selves in accomplishing their purpose because they have not just found something to live for but something to die for. They are prepared to pay the ultimate price with their lives because the cause they pursue is worth sacrificing for. Their lives transcend normalities; they are self-motivated to the extent that they may be perceived as a threat or burden to others.

The momentum of passionate individuals cannot be easily subdued. Threats and adverse conditions only serve to propel them further. They do not require ideal circumstances to move forward because passion is internally generated and remains unaffected by external conditions. These individuals do not rely on external stimuli to lift them when they fall; their passion is the force that keeps them rising. They exhibit steadfast determination, serving as their own incubators of courage, confidence, and competence.

Their strong sense of discipline ensures their consistent persistence, turning challenges into opportunities to break free from stagnation and comfort zones. They stand strong in the face of troubles or threats because their passion transcends even the fear of death. For passionate individuals, the pursuit of their vision consumes them to the point where they cannot stop, sleep well, or eat well until they have satisfied their commitment to making the vision a reality.

Those lacking passion may easily be discouraged by repeated failures, job losses, heartbreaks, emotional trauma, empty bank accounts, or a lack of external support. Passion, however, confronts every tragic circumstance with resilience, declaring, "Strike me down, kill me, but I will rise again and again." Passionate individuals wake up each morning with excitement, viewing each day's challenges as opportunities to move closer to their vision, a vision that surpasses any adversity they may face.

Passion entails a relentless determination to keep going, no matter how many times life knocks you down. It is a commitment to rising again and again, fueled by a goal so compelling that it outweighs the desire to quit. A life without passion may conform to expectations outwardly, but deep down, it is hurting and fulfilled. Passion is the eagerness to act immediately, to start pursuing a vision without delay, and the willingness to pay any price worth it, even with one's life, because the cause is deemed worthy.

KEYS TO RE-DISCOVERING THE PERSON YOU WERE MEANT TO BECOME

I have still not gotten over the fact that nothing is as elusive as purpose to the average human. They say there is no purpose to life, while others assert that life's purpose is the purpose you give it. Some say life's purpose is to wake up, take a bath, eat and drink, go to school, graduate, get a job, make love,

163

have children, wait until you are retired, and finally, have an appointment with death. Others say that is not all because there is more to life; you have to be happy, have fun, do what your heart wants, mind your own business, and enjoy the pleasures of life. Those who questions the systems that we seem they outsmart the world say purpose is a matrix to set you on the path of competition and conformity. Some religions say the purpose of life is to love, do good, be kind, be loving, be obedient, follow ethical and moral principles, engage in worship and prayer, and eventually go to Heaven for some. Others believe life's purpose is self-development, maintaining a good diet, building body muscles and shapes, dressing well, being money-conscious, and making more money. Some focus on learning about the history of life and linking it to the purpose of our lives. However, purpose remains elusive to many as they try to attach it to religion, school, jobs, relationships, zodiac signs, numerology, pleasures, and more.

As encapsulated above under "the inherent element of purpose," understanding your individual unique "why" or purpose should have all these inherent element in it which requires having a meeting with yourself. The "why" of your life is in the mind of God, the Creator of all things, who transmits it into images in the eyes of your mind. Re-discovering the "why" involves disintegrating the "what" of your life. Answering these questions may take days, challenging your daily routines, pushing you to a deep personal obligation, and prompting commitment. These interconnected questions are meant to introduce you to yourself, not others. The answers should merge like a puzzle, connecting to each other in a pattern,

164

evolving in the eyes of your mind for different seasons of your life, revealing what you are supposed to do. God reveals purpose gradually to prevent your mind from being blown away because you will completely denied it when it comes into picture all once.

Zero in now to have a meeting with yourself to re-capture the meaning of the existence for your life or purpose that God gave you. But before that, I would like you to meet with God first through prayer, my friend.

Prayer:

Heavenly Father, You are the Father of all humanity, and You are my Father. Your Name and Character are perfect.

Let Your ideas about the truth of the reason for my existence come into clearer view in the eyes of my mind, and let Your purpose for my life before the foundation of the world become my destined purpose, making my existence on Earth necessary.

Whatever You thought of me when You formed my physical body out of the dust of the ground is what I desire. I know that Your thoughts for me are good, and that You have a future planned for me to succeed and exceed my expectations.

Today, I re-dedicate my entire self to Your purpose for my existence and surrender my life to fulfilling Your purpose for my life in this my generation, impacting beneficially the succeeding generations. Re-veal to me the problem I was born to solve, what I was born to be known for, and what is worth living and

sacrificing my life for, making my existence necessary on this
planet Earth, before I take my last breath.

Let me live an effective life of possibility, and let me die satisfied
in my own spirit without wishing and regretting that I could live
back again. All thanks be to You Father-God, the Creator of all
things including my life.

A MEETING WITH YOURSELF TO RE-CAPTURING THE MEANING OF THE EXISTENCE FOR YOUR LIFE

Start by reflecting on your past, present, and future in a dedicated meeting with yourself. Take the time to answer questions related to these aspects of your life. Use a notebook, diary, computer, or any written medium that you would not easily misplace or damage. Keep in mind that these questions are interconnected, and your answers should align. If you notice they appears completely different from each other altogether, invest ample time in refining them until you are deeply convinced of each answer.

Prioritize questions with clear answers, refining those that seem less distinct as you go along. Be prepared for doubt, as some answers may challenge your existing beliefs, evoke fear, or surpass others' expectations of you. Embrace the possibility that your journey to becoming yourself may unravel old perceptions and confront aspects of yourself you have tried to avoid. What you thought you were not might clash with the true self emerging in your awareness.

Do not be surprised if your newfound understanding challenges preconceived notions about yourself. And at the end of it all, you have to be able to reduce all the responses to a word, or a phrase, or a sentence—thus, you should be able to simplify your entire life on this planet Earth to concide with one thing and that is your life's purpose. This process is a gateway to re-discovering God's purpose for your life. Embrace the discomfort, as it is part of the journey toward becoming yourself. Now, embark on this journey to meet yourself for the first time.

1. What do I most desire to ensure the world is save from?

It is about the burning desire deep within you to ensure the safety of the world. It is about your unyielding craving for progress, rectifying historical inaccuracies, reconstruction, and restructuring – a hunger that cannot be satisfied by any alternatives. It revolves around what truly matters to you, a passion that refuses to be appeased until it is realized. This hunger is not just any hunger; it is the hunger to save the world, encompassing the systems of order that govern everything on our planet – from your immediate surroundings to society, nation, continent, and the entire globe, encompassing all life, including humanity. What is it that you genuinely want to save the world from?

To "save" denotes a transformation from one state of being to another, but not just any change. We are not referring to changes that corrupt, destroy, oppress, inflict harm, or starve lives. Instead, it is about the change that uplifts and advances things towards their improved, correct, original state. What change are you relentlessly yearning for? It is that singular change that prevents you from finding comfort and fulfillment until it is accomplished.

Throughout my entire life, I have not yet encountered a single person who does not wish for some form of change in the world. We are inherently destined to be agents of change by God, a clear testament to our purpose. What is it about the world that you are deeply passionate about changing, leaving an insatiable hunger within you? You are not meant to change everything; there is a specific thing you were born to change in the world before drawing your last breath. What is that change, my friend?

2. What triggers anger in me that becomes a constructive force in my reactions?

What sparks a positive, constructive anger in you that drives your actions? It is those circumstances around you that, whenever you encounter or hear about them, stir up a consistent sense of anger within you. These circumstances do not allow you to simply mind your own business. Instead, they trigger hormones, activating your entire body and instilling a deep personal commitment to immediately address or devise a constructive plan to resolve them.

Friend, what is it about that anger that compels you to abandon everything at hand and rush to solve the issue? This type of anger is not destructive; rather, it is a constructive force that aims to alleviate suffering, preserve, protect, promote, and enhance lives. It is not the kind of anger that drives revenge, inflicts pain on others, or leads to a torrent of insults in speech or writing. It does not involve using weapons to harm or take lives. This arousal of anger is not disruptive or chaotic; instead, it taps into a form of strength that empowers you to rectify wrongs.

What are the circumstances that trigger such strong reactions in you? These are precisely the issues you were born to solve, making your existence important on this planet. If it were not for these circumstances, you would not exist, as your presence would be superfluous to the lives around you and the world at large. What is that anger that prompts you to forsake the pleasures of life and resolve to make things right, even if it means dropping out of school, dedicating months or years to study a specific program, or leaving a job that hinders your ability to address the issue head-on? What is that unique anger in your spirit that consistently pulls you away from the comforts of life to actively construct solutions until the task is completed?

God is introducing you to the problem you were born to solve. What is that ongoing circumstance that taps into your anger, making you constructive? It is the specific problem that gives your existence purpose, importance, and inherently uncovers within you the potential to solve it. This is the particular question of life on Earth that you were born to answer.

3.What instills the deepest fear in me, yet when confronted, brings me alive?

These are the things you know deep within your spirit you could do better, but your lack of knowledge on them scares you the most. What is that thing you have not experienced much yet, but when you tackle it, you know you were built for it? You have the necessary potential within you, but you are on the blank side of it.

Remember, whatever you were born to do, you have not done it before; you are like a virgin to it, leaving you with a sense of fear. And you are always reluctant about doing it, always imagining yourself doing it, yet it always instills some holy fear in you because you do not know the processes you are going to take or go through. What is that fear that you know that emptiness within you could only be filled from?

This fear is the road you always want to avoid on your way to your destiny. It is the expectations of others, be it your loved ones, but they still do not get you right. It is the fear of stopping pleasing people's goals for your life and becoming the center of your own choices and decisions without accommodating theirs in yours. It is the fear you want to always free yourself from, and not being able to free yourself from it is what leaves some form of emptiness within you.

What is that fear you always want to free yourself from? That fear is what introduces you to yourself. What has defeated many people from becoming themselves is fear; it is self-nurtured of nonexistent realities to the one whose mind conceives it. Fear has this capacity that can let you betray yourself for nothing. Fear is the misuse of your imagination power. Fear is not something in some of us; it is in everyone as we take the path we want to avoid, not because of the dark we see there but the light that shines to introduce ourselves to ourselves that frightens most. If you go on that path you want to avoid, you will liberate yourself as well as liberate others too. If you stop having faith in fear and place that faith in yourself, you will be free from misjudgment of others, school grades, expectations, opinions, manifest what you are capable of, and become yourself. What is that deepest fear holding you back?

4. What action do I feel most sorry for not taking in my life?

What is that action you deeply regret not taking in your life? This pertains to a longstanding aspiration that refuses to fade, persisting in your imagination without wavering. It represents a desire you have not shared with others, envisioning a version of yourself engaged in this pursuit. This longing surfaces in various settings—be it at school, work, social gatherings, or even in solitude, like a persistent thought in your mind. Whether you are in a bustling crowd, a quiet corner, a car, kitchen, bathroom, or anywhere else, you find yourself yearning for this unfulfilled vision.

This unfulfilled vision haunts your thoughts not only during waking hours but also infiltrates your nights, keeping you awake as you mentally wander through memories, imagining what could have been. It is a profound desire to contribute meaningfully to others. Even amidst busyness, this unfulfilled vision asserts itself, tugging at your heartstrings, urging you to redirect your focus and engage in what truly matters to you.

What is this unspoken desire that consistently evokes regret for not pursuing it more earnestly? It is the one thing that, despite being overshadowed by life's obligations, resurfaces persistently in your mind's eye. What action, driven by a childhood passion, beckons you to break free from the constraints of your current activities and dive into the fulfillment of a vision that has stood the test of time?

5. What can I occupy myself with that would not make me feel like I am wasting my time?

What activities can you engage in that would not leave you feeling like you are wasting time? If life equates to time, what would you choose to spend your time on?

It is about pursuing what truly matters to you, finding joy in the moments you once thought were wasted. If you do not find fulfillment in certain activities you are engaging your time in now, then you are squandering your life and neglecting what genuinely matters to you.

What activities bring you joy and make you feel alive? It is about dedicating time to pursuits that uplift your spirit, not only bringing you alive but also infusing significance into the lives of those around you.

What is that one thing that captivates you so much that you would not want to retire from it? What can you spend your time on without a sense of wasting it? It is the pursuit that not only does not dampen your spirit but consistently provides mental, spiritual, and physical fulfillment. What would you commit your entire life to without contemplating retirement?

6. What engagements have I found that reignite my enthusiasm and joy for life?

Consider pondering moments in your past that brought you immense joy and enthusiasm. Now, live in the present, taking a moment to observe your current state. Step outside of yourself and project into the future, envisioning activities that bring you a deep sense of inner peace. These are the pursuits that, when engaged in, dispel feelings of depression, sorrow, and inadequacy. They instill a sense of self-worth not only within yourself but also resonate with others and the world.

Explore these fulfilling experiences through volunteer work, where you invest your time without expecting payment. Delve into your leisure activities and hobbies, identifying those that offer greater satisfaction than your job, even if they do not come with a paycheck. Pinpoint the pursuits that you find so inherently rewarding that you would continue doing them even without recognition, thanks, or financial compensation. Reflecting on these aspects re-introduces you to the purpose for your life that God, the Creator of all things, gave you that brings fulfillment to your life.

These engagements serve as a compass, guiding you towards a life fulfilling life, irrespective of external validation. The essence lies in the inherent rewards derived from these activities. So, take a moment to contemplate and re-discover these sources of fulfillment that reignite your enthusiasm and joy for life.

7. What overshadows the pleasures that life offers me?

Certain aspects consume your entire existence to the extent that you forget about life's pleasures—engaging in multiple sexual encounters, attending events and parties, watching television, being online, immersing yourself in current trends, substance abuse, and adopting the latest fashion styles. It is about the inner conviction you have that makes you choose to enjoy the prison of your vision so that you can live a stress-free life in the days to come, rather than enjoying the palace of your pleasures and regretting later because it could not fill the void of emptiness within you.

What specific activity do you desire to engage in rather than merely indulging in life's pleasures? These pursuits lead to a profound conviction that there are actions you ought to avoid, prompting you to live not just in the present but with an eye on the future. They shape your life priorities, emphasizing the importance of addressing the most crucial matters first. This framework establishes personal principles that guide you, discouraging you from sacrificing your vision for the fleeting allure of pleasures. It does not diminish the enjoyment of life's pleasures; instead, it elevates you to a level where you realize your comfort zone can be more dangerous which is backed up by an inner conviction compelling you to break barriers, enabling others to reach greater heights and alter the course of history because something is wrong.

This conviction is rooted in a sense of responsibility towards your generations, an urgency to alleviate their suffering. It transcends mere political leadership positions, coveted titles, dreams of amassing wealth, or any offerings life might present, as these could eventually undermine your commitment to the well-being of your generation and those to come.

Friend, what kind of responsibility do you sense in your spirit towards your generation and the succeeding ones? It is not just a fleeting emotion; rather, it is a desire more potent than the pleasures life offers. What specific undertaking consistently overshadows the allure of life's pleasures? Even if you feel for enjoyment, this sense of responsibility swiftly extinguishes that feeling, akin to a match's flame being extinguished.

8. What gives me the greatest inspiration, leading to my own capacity to inspire?

An unexpected way for you to be introduced to yourself by God, the Creator of all things, is going through what I call the hell of life. The average person does not want to experience these moments in their life; we even try to pray them away because we see them as detrimentally opposed to what we desire. Whatever you are experiencing, especially the bad, is not happening to you; it is happening for you.

One of the most common ways to be introduced to yourself is by becoming a victim of a moment or circumstances. These moments are often the most challenging in your life; they make us question whether God is still with us, working for us, and listening to our prayers. They prompt us to question why God allows so many evil to happen. It makes us question why there are hardships, failures, broken promises, disappointments, accidents, breakups, divorces, betrayals, lies, hospitalizations, imprisonment, unemployment, abuse, misuse, and cheating.

Remember, these moments may be what divinity chooses to direct you towards the self you were born to become.

Consider your own significant life experiences, those moments that shaped you. What lessons did you extract from them, and how have they influenced your character? By sharing these experiences, you have the potential to guide others on their life journeys, helping them navigate challenges and make sound decisions for their future.

Think about the moments you would not wish upon anyone else – the hardships, failures, and disappointments. What experiences do you believe are worth sharing to assist others in moving forward in life? Perhaps there is a particular experience that has inspired you to make a living out of it, to impact not only your generation but also those that follow.

God's intention is for you to harness the knowledge gained from these experiences and release it to the world, fostering improvement, drawing out the best in others, and challenging them to step into their own purposes. What is the profound inspiration embedded in your spirit, given by God, the Creator of all things, that propels you to inspire others? Identify that calling, that purpose, which makes you certain that you were born to dedicate your entire life to it.

---

9. What sets me apart from the norm in terms of what I do?

WHAT MAKES YOU STAND out in what you do? It is that thing you engage in without feeling threatened or negative, because you are so secure in yourself that you not only continue to do it but also strive to help and teach others to excel in it. It is the activity that, when you see someone else doing it, you find yourself identifying with them on a deep level, feeling more alive.

This special pursuit is not just a job; it is something you can not imagine retiring from. It is an integral part of your life, inseparable from your being. There is no disconnect between you and this activity. What is this one thing you want to share with others? You are so confident in your abilities that you believe no one else can do it quite like you. You envision your legacy living on even after you take your last breath because of this unique aspect of yourself.

On the flip side, what is that one thing you were born to be known for? What do you want to be recognized for, and how do you plan to dedicate your entire life to perfecting it and teaching others to surpass your achievements? Often, external validation comes in the form of compliments. What is that particular compliment that solidifies your conviction about doing something, especially when you have kept it a secret or lacked prior experience or training?

Embarking on your distinct purpose might attract criticism and threats from various sources – be it parents, family, friends, or society at large. Yet, these challenges signify that you are venturing into uncharted territories, attempting the seemingly impossible. When faced with such opposition, you might find yourself on the path of fulfilling God's purpose for your life.

What is the activity that, despite receiving criticism or threats, only strengthens your conviction? What sets you apart from the norm becomes clearer when you face challenges for pursuing your unique calling. It is about re-discovering God's purpose for your life, something that differentiates you from everyone else on this planet.

So, what is that thing you do, and maybe you have encountered compliments, criticism, or threats, but deep within, you are more convinced than ever that this is exactly what you were born to do and be known for? It is this conviction that truly sets you apart from the crowd.

10. What would be my course of action, if I were certain that only death could stop me?

This question encompasses the preceding nine questions, and here is why: If what you have typed on your computer, or penned on the paper, or book does not warrant your readiness to sacrifice your life for it, then it is not deserving of you living it. If you lack the self-conviction to die for it, you do not truly believe in it. Dying for what you are convinced you were born to do delves beyond the literal meaning of death; It is about possessing a steadfast passion and certainty that failure cannot impede your progress.

Those elusive grades on your examination certificate do not dictate your capabilities or limitations. It is about being convicted that no threat of death, sickness, job loss, position of power, or change in title can deter you. It is about being certain that neither physical nor spiritual weapons can sever your commitment to pursuing the purpose you believe is God-given, and that you are meant to live and die for it. If what you have documented lacks the essence that you are willing to lay down your life for it, it is the greatest testament that it not God's purpose for your life. God's purpose instills both conviction and passion, creating an internalized death to compromising but an abundant life to commitment that transcends your environment and reactions to what is happening around you.

This conviction goes beyond being "possessed"; it prompts others to question the origin of your steadfast passion, leading them to marvel at your readiness to sacrifice everything for your cause. It compels you to become one with your purpose, intertwining your daily activities with it to the point where separation becomes inconceivable. This question revolves around the commitment to shed other aspects of yourself and fully embrace the self that aligns with your passion. It boils down to the willingness to die for what you believe in.

Below are some individuals who are integrated with their life's purpose and have expressed their passion for it:

> *"When the hour came, Jesus and his disciples reclined at the table. And he said to them, 'I have eagerly desired to eat this Passover with you before I suffer.* **For I tell you, I will not eat it again until it finds fulfillment in the Kingdom of God... For even I, the Son of Man, came here not to be served but to serve others, and to give my life as a ransom for many.'"**
> *—Jesus Christ (Luke 22:14-16; Mark 10:45)*

*"What anyone else dares to boast about—I am speaking as a fool—I also dare to boast about. Are they Hebrews? So am I. Are they Israelites? So am I. Are they Abraham's descendants? So am I. Are they servants of Christ? (I am out of my mind to talk like this.) I am more. I have worked much harder, been in prison more frequently, been flogged more severely, and been exposed to death again and again. Five times I received from the Jews the forty lashes minus one. Three times I was beaten with rods, once I was stoned, three times I was shipwrecked, I spent a night and a day in the open sea, I have been constantly on the move. I have been in danger from rivers, in danger from bandits, in danger from my own countrymen, in danger from Gentiles; in danger in the city, in danger in the country, in danger at sea; and in danger from false brothers. I have labored and toiled and have often gone without sleep; I have known hunger and thirst and have often gone without food; I have been cold and naked. Besides everything else, I face daily the pressure of my concern for all the Churches... **I eagerly expect and hope that I will in no way be ashamed, but will have sufficient courage so that now as always Christ will be exalted in my body, whether by life or by death. For to me, to live is Christ and to die is gain...** For I am not ashamed of the Gospel (good news) of Christ, for it is God's power working unto salvation [for deliverance from eternal death] to everyone who believes with a personal trust and a confident surrender and firm reliance, to the Jew first*

and also to the Greek,... For I am already being poured out like a drink offering, and the time has come for my departure. I have fought the good fight, I have finished the race, I have kept the faith."—Paul of Tarsus (2 Corinthians 11:22-28; Romans 1:16; Philippians 1:20-21; 2 Timothy 4:6-7).

"I have fought against white domination and I have fought against black domination. I have cherished the ideal of a democratic and free society in which all persons live together in harmony and with equal opportunities. **It is an ideal which I hope to live for and to achieve. But if needs be, it is an ideal for which I am prepared to die."**—*Nelson Mandela*

"I have often inquired of myself what great principle or idea it was that kept this Confederacy [Union] so long together....It was that which gave promise that in due time the weight would be lifted from the shoulders of all men. This is a sentiment embodied in the Declaration of Independence.... **I have said nothing but what I am willing to live by and, if it be the pleasure of Almighty God, die by."** —*Abraham Lincoln*

Re-discovering your purpose in life is about recognizing what you were meant to do and fully embracing it with passion. Without passion, your purpose remains elusive, leaving you feeling disconnected from your self. When you are passionate about something, it ignites a fire within you, driving you to pursue your goals with unwavering determination.

Purpose is not just about going through the motions; it is about finding deep fulfillment in what you do. If you are merely going through the motions without feeling that sense of passion, then you have not re-discovered your purpose yet. Instead, you are living a life that lacks authenticity—is illusive, just existing.

When you align with your purpose, you feel a sense of inner peace and satisfaction. It is as if everything falls into place, and you become unstoppable in pursuing your vision. Challenges may arise, but your passion fuels your determination, pushing you to overcome any obstacles that stand in your way.

From now until your final breath on this earth, I want you to deeply contemplate the responses you have provided for the ten questions mentioned, whether they are stored on your computer, written in a book, or on a piece of paper and reduce all of them to a word or a sentence—thus, you are simplifying your entire life on this planet Earth to concide with one thing and that is your life's purpose. Take heed of the word, or phrase, or the sentence you have reduced to, dedicating time each day to revisit and ponder it, until it is etched into your mind so deeply that it become an inseparable part of you. Visualize it vividly, seeing it in the recesses of your mind's eye as you go about your daily routines—whether it is brushing your teeth, in the bathroom, studying, forging relationships, during tough times in prison or hospital, during moments of rest or meals, and even in moments of despair, failure, heartbreak, job loss, or rejection. Let it guide you in every decision, big or small, shaping your perspective, influencing your choices and be your greatest motivator.

I assure you that what you sees in the eyes of your mind will come true, although it may not be immediate. This is because the ideas that God has implanted in your mind are truthful seeds and will come to fruition at the appointed time. Once this time reach, your life will become revolutionary not just for yourself, but the people around you and the world as a whole.

Chapter 6: Principles To Think About Before You Take Your Last Breath

———

1. Nothing always strikes me as how we cherish ourselves more than others, yet we value their opinions about us more than our own. Start afresh by assessing each person's opinion based on who they are, not who you are. Be convinced living as if this is your second chance, detached from the expectations of humanity. Embrace your new life as if you were already dead to societal expectations.

2. Live with the mindset of a dying person who is on borrowed time, liberate yourself from the grip of others' opinions, and do not delay anything that brings you fulfillment. Polish the details of your life daily, recognizing that each day's experiences are distinct from your life's essence. Consider what you do with these experiences, rather than letting them define your existence.

3. Trust in yourself; perceive every occurrence as a divine progression, steering you towards a necessary path, even if it seems like an obstacle. Have faith that it is God's way of propelling you toward the life He intended for you. Live that purpose, and success and unexpected greatness will unfold in your everyday moments.

4. *Purpose is the conviction of a vision that is created by inspiration, which becomes a passion for living.*

5. Your convictions are not mere abstract concepts; they are the lifeblood of your belief system. They define who you are, what you stand for, and how you engage with the world. They are the moral fiber that holds together the fabric of your character.

6. Your conviction is a belief in yourself. Your entire life is controlled and determined by your belief system about yourself. It is impossible to separate your life from your belief system. Your conviction is what bounces you forward even when you want to go back; it is a willingness and capacity to walk alone even when the entire world is against you. Your conviction is a certainty that you are unique and necessary to the world.

7. Your conviction is a deep seated belief that, you are not a copy of anyone else. It is genuine confidence based on your natural ability, a sense of inherent significant, and the knowledge that there is something you need to do without external urging. No one else can do what makes your existence necessary. This conviction quells fear, instills a confidence not commonly found, and may appear to come from somewhere else in the eyes of many. This conviction is often mistaken for arrogance by the insecure. It revolves around your belief about yourself, a belief that you have rediscovered what you need to do, always vivid in the eyes of your mind.

8. Your cherished conviction transforms into a vivid

vision in the eyes of your mind, or subconscious mind, or heart, not merely a visual perception. This vision is exclusive to you; only you are intended to see it. Even if those around you or the world fail to see what you envision, do not abandon it. Every vision has its first believer, and that is the individual who has faith in it.

9. Your vision can never makes you insensitive to others; instead, it contributes to the well-being of humanity, upholding moral principles and safeguarding lives.

10. Purpose is an assignment with a divine touch.

11. Individuals living with passion find themselves prisoners of their visions, risking their lives to fulfill them. Their resilience stands firm even when faced with unexpected and repeated storms of life, including failed examinations, painful breakups, emotional trauma, life imprisonment, serious health issues, setbacks, mistakes, job loss, loss of position, and more.

12. Passionate individuals are willing to invest their entire selves in accomplishing their purpose because they have not just found something to live for but something to die for. They are prepared to pay the ultimate price with their lives because the cause they pursue is worth sacrificing for. Their lives transcend normalities; they are self-motivated to the extent that they may be perceived as a threat or burden to others.

13. The momentum of passionate individuals cannot be easily subdued. Threats and adverse conditions only serve to propel them further. They do not require ideal circumstances to move forward because passion

is internally generated and remains unaffected by external conditions. These individuals do not rely on external stimuli to lift them when they fall; their passion is the force that keeps them rising. They exhibit steadfast determination, serving as their own incubators of courage, confidence, and competence.

14. A life without passion may conform to expectations outwardly, but deep down, it is hurting and fulfilled.

CHAPTER

7

Understanding
The Life You Were Meant To Live

———

The greatest personal revelation in life is that while your purpose is chosen by God, the Creator of all things, the ultimate fulfillment of that purpose rests squarely upon your own will power. When we observe the turmoil in the stock market, the unrest on a global scale, the debates surrounding fundamental human rights, the discussions on nuclear arms, the precariousness of economic stability, and the upheaval caused by industrial strikes, it seems likely that many individuals have lost sight of the significance of fulfilling their purpose. Instead, they become preoccupied with the need to be important, inadvertently contributing to the chaotic problems plaguing our world.

Through the years of my life, I have sat under the feet of life, still a student of life and being taught that the most important thing on Earth is the fulfilment or completion of one's purpose. I much prefer to encapsulate in the simple yet profound notion of living immediately, effectively, and dying satisfactory without regretting one could live back again. Life, in its wisdom, continues to teach me this invaluable lesson.

In effect, acknowledging that our purpose is divinely ordained does not absolve us of responsibility; rather, it empowers us to actively engage in the fulfillment of that purpose. It is incumbent upon each individual to prioritize the realization of their purpose over the pursuit of personal acclaim or status. Failure to do so not only detracts from one's own fulfillment but also contributes to the larger societal issues we face.

To live immediately, effectively, and without regret requires a conscious commitment to discerning and pursuing our purpose with unwavering dedication. It demands that we resist the allure of superficial distractions and cultivate a steadfast focus on what truly matters. In doing so, we not only enrich our own lives but also create a ripple effect of positivity and transformation in the world.

The ramifications of neglecting our life purpose are manifold and far-reaching. When individuals prioritize being more important over authentic fulfillment, the fabric of society begins to fray. Economic instability, social unrest, and geopolitical tensions are symptomatic of this deeper malaise—a collective disconnection from our inherent purpose and the values that underpin it.

Conversely, when individuals embrace their purpose wholeheartedly, the world makes them important because they are catalysts for positive change. Their actions are imbued with meaning and significance, inspiring others to follow suit. This ripple effect has the potential to transcend boundaries, cultures, and generations, fostering a more harmonious and equitable world for all.

In light of these reflections, it is incumbent upon each of us to pause and reflect on the trajectory of our lives. Are we living in alignment with our purpose, or have we been sidetracked by the pursuit of fleeting desires? Are we contributing positively to the world around us, or are we inadvertently perpetuating its problems through our own apathy or self-interest? The will power to choose whether to fulfill our purpose or not lies in our very hands, not God.

THE POWER OF YOUR WILL

God is fully committed to making sure you fulfill your purpose. He has invested in the purpose He gave you, marshalling all spiritual forces, including angels and even the enemy, to ensure its completion. So, even when you feel like you have nothing, do not worry—God is still committed and will provide what you need, when and where you need it. He is more committed to your purpose than you are. He not only gave you the purpose but also has the plan for you to succeed in living it, because your success matters to Him. He is already prepared everything you need before you even existed on this planet Earth.

Paul of Tarsus expressed this idea, saying, *"Praise be to the God and Father of our Lord Jesus Christ, who has blessed us in the heavenly realms with every spiritual blessing in Christ. For He chose us in Him before the creation of the world to be holy and blameless in His sight in love. He predestined us to be adopted as His sons through Jesus Christ, in accordance with His pleasure and will" (Ephesians 1:3-5).* This shows that God has done everything out of love for humanity, ensuring our success.

Even though you may face challenges that do not feel good or look good, remember that God has a purpose for everything. He is setting you up to make a difference in the world. He

191

knows what you are going through and will ensure you come out of it. Nothing catches God, the Creator of all things, as a surprise. You have been chosen for this purpose, and you are the best person to work it out from the unseen of Heaven to the seen of the seen of this planet Earth.

However, the paradox is whether you succeed or fail ultimately depends on your cooperation with God's will. You have the choice to live according to His purpose, where He takes full responsibility for your success, or to pursue your own purpose, where success depends solely on your actions.

So, God grants each of us, humanity, a potent yet perilous gift – the power of will. This inherent ability distinguishes us from mere automatons, allowing us to shape our lives according to our own will and desires rather than predetermined programming. Unlike robots, which function solely based on preprogrammed instructions, we possess the capacity to make choices, to even deviate from the path set before us. While this autonomy is undoubtedly a blessing, it also carries immense risks.

The essence of this gift lies in its capacity that God, the Creator of all things, enable us two options—either to choose or choose against His will for your life. This is where its danger truly manifests. With our willpower, we can even refuse to be what we were born to be, reject the existence of God entirely, dismissing the notion of absolute morality and purpose in life. We may even opt for purposes divergent from the purpose intended for us by our God, the Creator of all things, pursuing material wealth or personal ambitions instead. In doing so, we jeopardize not only our own well-being of being peace with ourselves but also the harmony of the world around us.

It is imperative to recognize the magnitude of this gift bestowed upon us. While it grants us freedom and agency, it also demands responsibility. Our choices hold the power to shape not only our own destinies but also the fabric of society. Therefore, let us reflect upon the weight of our desires, decisions and strive to align them with the greater purpose intended by our God, the Creator of all things.

In effect, our willpower is a double-edged sword, capable of both great good and great harm. It is up to us to wield it wisely, acknowledging the inherent risks while embracing the boundless potential it offers. Through mindfulness and discernment, we can harness this gift to fulfill our purpose and contribute positively to the world around us.

The Unchangingness of the Purpose of Your Life

You are not just a random mix of sperm and egg. Your existence on Earth is not a coincidence; it is part of a grand plan. The Earth needs you so much that your presence is important for the world to function properly. You are not a mistake of biology; no one on this planet is. Your birth serves a purpose, a purpose set by God, the Creator of all things, and your purpose is unchanging and essential, even if life's challenges make it hard to believe.

Your purpose is not just to pass time on Earth; it is a mission given to you by God. It is more significant than anything else, shaping the very fabric of your being. Success or failure, accolades or criticism, none of it compares to the importance of fulfilling your purpose. Even if circumstances seem daunting or you have made mistakes, your purpose remains untarnished.

Your journey may be tough, surrounded by people who do not understand or appreciate you. But as long as you stay true to yourself, your purpose will guide you through. Every experience, good or bad, is preparing you for your destiny. Your purpose transcends your current situation; it is bigger than your age, achievements, or setbacks.

Do not dwell on past mistakes or let fear of the future hold you back. Your purpose is permanent, a beacon of hope amid life's uncertainties. Never let your passion outrun your patience in God. Stay patient and trust in the timing of your purpose. Build a strong relationship with the Creator of all things, for it is in alignment with God that you will find fulfillment.

Failures and problems may come your way, but they do not define you. Your purpose is more powerful than any obstacle you face. Embrace your journey, with all its ups and downs, knowing that each challenge is a stepping stone towards your purpose. Your failures will be turned into testimonies, fueling the revolution of your destiny.

Even when you feel used or unappreciated, hold onto your purpose with pride. You have survived difficult times and persevered through misunderstandings, never losing sight of your true calling. Your purpose is your strength, a constant presence in a world of change.

Perhaps you have been stuck in a job for many years that makes you feel down, overwhelms you, and does not pay enough, so you need to juggle two or three jobs just to get by. But do not worry, God reassures you that everything is still okay. The reason He put you on this Earth has not been cancelled. All you need to do is align yourself with Him.

Similarly, if you have dropped out of school due to lack of discipline, or if you find yourself in challenging situations like the hospital, prison, or any unsafe environment where your life feels at risk, God wants you to know that He is still watching over you. He is still committed to the purpose He has for you. You just need to cooperate with Him, rather than focusing on the negative circumstances around you.

Even the toughest challenges or fears you are facing right now could be stepping stones towards fulfilling your purpose. Often, we find ourselves learning important lessons through experiences we would rather avoid. God, the Creator of all things, has a specific path He wants to guide you on to fulfill your purpose, and He will lead you there in His own time.

In simpler terms, if you are unsure about what to do with your life right now, God may allow you to go through different experiences—good and bad, mundane and challenging—to ultimately guide you towards your purpose.

Let these words burn in your psyche, a reminder of your inherent worth and purpose. Never forget that you are here for a reason, and that reason is something to be cherished and celebrated.

Factors that might throw you off your life's purpose

Most often, we are not able to live up to the climax of the fulfilment of our life's purpose. We start well, but the finishing is so hard. Some do not even start at all because the start itself tends to frighten and threaten them to death. As I sat down to observe life carefully, not just once, I have been able to note down the major factors that might throw one off their life's purpose, and they are as follows:

1. Chains of expectations.

From the moment we enter this world, we are assigned a country, a family, and a predefined role to fulfill. This predetermined path extends to the quality of our thoughts, burdened by a web of expectations dictating what we should do to find inner peace. This burden is most keenly felt within our immediate family, where those who care for us often pose the greatest threat to our individual life's purpose.

They assert, "I've provided for you since your arrival, fought your battles, and imparted you with wisdom. Don't presume to be smarter than me to figure out what's best for your life. I walked this Earth before you, and I know better." Some even go as far as to threaten withdrawal of support if we do not conform to their desires: "If you refuse to comply with my wishes, I'll withhold everything from you. No schooling, no financial support, no encouragement for your dreams. You'll no longer be my child. I disown you."

In this emotional dungeon, our visions are imprisoned, forcing us to forsake our selves and adopt the personas they have constructed for us. This coercion is perilous and should not be underestimated. To parents especially, I caution: Parenthood does not equate to ownership of your child's life, nor does it confer omniscience regarding their destiny. It is imperative to listen to your children, cultivate intimacy to understand their capabilities, and seek God's guidance to figure out their life's purpose. Presuming to know what is best for them based on your experiences or others' is fallacious. Allow your children to feel secure in their own existence. Do not let your past traumas dictate their future. Your role is to nurture their journey towards re-discovering and fulfilling their life's purpose, ensuring they do not stray onto paths dictated by others.

2. Cultural norms.

In our world, we have been taught not to trust our own instincts, not to have conviction in ourselves. It is the harsh truth of today's reality. Our society, it is a mental prison, designed to crush our spirits.

When someone surrenders to their circumstances, to the powers that be, it is like saying, "I give up, I can't fight anymore." It is a sure sign that their conviction has been shattered, replaced by the oppressive history that says they are not capable of making a meaningful impact.

The trouble is, we have all internalized this idea, unknowingly becoming passive in pursuing our life's purposes. But passivity is not natural; it is something we have been conditioned to accept. I have struggled with that same demon of "norm", seeing it as a form of mediocrity, where we are not allowed to stand out. But it is time to reject the norms imposed upon us and declare, "I don't belong to this culture anymore; my culture comes from God, the Creator of all things."

Deep within us lies the potential to change the world, but too often, we bury it under layers of societal conditioning. We are taught to suppress our inner voices, to never push back, to simply go along with the status quo. They feed us words like "cooperate" and "be submissive," all while secretly aiming to stifle our potential. We are like oxen, harnessed and controlled by threats, intimidation, and false promises of power. They instill fear to keep us in line, warning of pain if we dare to step out of bounds. But I believe that as you read this, you will cast off those chains and reclaim your sense of conviction and self-determination.

Let the conviction within you about yourself outweigh any doubts others may have about you. It is time to reclaim your passion and prioritize your own opinion of yourself over the judgments of others. Culture, in essence, is just the collective mindset of a society. It is time to break free from that mindset and forge your own path towards fulfilling your life's purpose.

3. Imposter syndrome.

It is important to grasp that what has happened before is likely to happen again, and there is nothing entirely new under the sun, as stated in Ecclesiastes 1:9. Therefore, what truly counts is how you carry out your purpose. Do not become overly concerned or troubled if your purpose resembles that of someone else; what truly matters is how you execute it. It is natural to feel intimidated when you see others whose purposes seem similar to yours achieving great success, overshadowing your own emerging efforts. However, it is crucial to remember that while the objective may be similar, the method intended for you by God, the Creator of all things, is unique to you. Keep this thought firmly rooted in your mind to avoid doubting your abilities, skills, or the potential impact of your accomplishments on the world.

Avoid persistently fearing being perceived as incompetent simply because you have not yet attained the level of success you desire. Do not let the fear of failure or inadequacy hold you back from taking risks and seizing opportunities for growth. Refrain from attributing your achievements or potential achievements solely to luck, chance, or external factors, without acknowledging the effort and determination you have put in. Success ultimately hinges on your effort and belief in yourself, so let your conviction about your abilities outweigh any doubts others may have about you. Unless if it turns other way round, you will submit to what the naysayers and the experts says.

4. Ego-driven desires.

Being driven by our ego is not necessarily a negative thing. It is what propels us to constantly strive for self-improvement, seeking to add value and significance to ourselves. This desire for recognition and enhancement often leads us to pursue paths that we believe will elevate our status and contribute positively to the world. However, when this drive is not rooted in our own genuine beliefs but rather influenced by external forces within our social circle, it can become problematic.

Within our social circles, there are typically two types of people: those who are for us and those who are against us. Those who are for us are individuals who share our values, connect with us deeply, provide encouragement, and genuinely want to see us succeed. These may include family members, favorite teachers, close friends, mentors, or admired figures whose opinions we value. Their compliments and suggestions, while well-intentioned, may sometimes lead us astray if they do not align with our convictions and visions.

Conversely, there are those who opposes everything about us are those who are against us. These people may undermine our confidence and discourage us from pursuing our visions. They may point out perceived shortcomings or limitations, attempting to dissuade us from paths they deem unsuitable based on their own biases or agendas. Their negative remarks can either deflate our vision or ignite a determination to prove them wrong.

It is crucial for individuals to discern between these influences and evaluate whether they resonate with their convictions and visions. While compliments and advice from well-meaning supporters can provide valuable insights, blindly following them without considering their alignment with ourselves can lead to feelings of emptiness and dissatisfaction in the long run.

Many successful individuals have achieved external acclaim and material wealth but still feel unfulfilled because their pursuits were not in line with their authentic selves but other selves. It is essential for young people to recognize that fulfillment comes from pursuing paths that align with their passions, rather than solely seeking external validation or conforming to others' expectations.

Furthermore, it is important not to let both experts and naysayers deter us from our visions or succumb to societal pressures to fit into predetermined roles. Believing in ourselves and staying true to our inner convictions, even in the face of criticism or doubt, is key to finding satisfaction and fulfillment in life.

Ultimately, individuals must weigh the opinions of both supporters (those who are for them) and detractors (those who are against them) within their social circles, considering whether their voices aligns with their own sense of purpose and fulfillment. Straying from one's authentic path to satisfy others' expectations or prove them wrong may lead to temporary validation but will likely result in a lack of fulfillment and a sense of purposelessness in the long term.

5. Pitfalls of perfectionism.

In the quest for excellence and the pursuit of one's life purpose, striving for flawless execution and high standards is often seen as a commendable attitude. However, the concept of perfectionism can often derail individuals from their intended path, leading them astray from fulfilling their life's purpose. Perfectionism, while initially appearing to be a positive trait, can manifest in various detrimental ways, ultimately hindering progress and causing individuals to lose sight of their visions.

One of the ways in which perfectionism can impede the pursuit of one's life purpose is through an excessive self-criticism. When individuals hold themselves to impossibly high standards, they become overly critical of their own work, constantly finding fault and flaws even in their achievements. This self-imposed scrutiny can breed feelings of inadequacy and demotivation, ultimately stifling creativity and progress towards one's life purpose.

Moreover, perfectionism often brings about an intense pressure to succeed, often within unrealistic timeframes. Individuals driven by perfectionism may feel compelled to achieve perfection on their first attempt, fearing failure or criticism from others. This relentless pursuit of immediate success can lead to burnout and exhaustion, diverting attention away from the essence of one's life purpose.

Another pitfall of perfectionism is the tendency to fixate on minute details at the expense of the bigger picture. When individuals become overly focused on achieving perfection in every aspect of their work or performance, they risk losing sight of the overarching goals and objectives that define their life's purpose. This tunnel vision prevents individuals from adapting to changing circumstances and exploring alternative avenues for growth and fulfillment.

Furthermore, perfectionism often breeds a paralyzing fear of making mistakes. Rather than embracing failures as opportunities for learning and growth, perfectionists are consumed by the fear of not meeting their own impossibly high standards. This fear-based mindset stifles innovation and creativity, as individuals become more concerned with avoiding mistakes than seizing opportunities for progress towards their life purpose.

Additionally, perfectionism can lead individuals to postpone action indefinitely in search of the "perfect" time or conditions. This procrastination prevents individuals from taking the necessary steps towards fulfilling their life's purpose, as they wait for external circumstances to align perfectly with their unrealistic expectations. This perpetual waiting game only serves to delay progress and dampen the passion and drive necessary for pursuing one's life purpose.

In essence, the key to overcoming the pitfalls of perfectionism lies in embracing imperfection and taking action in the present moment. Rather than waiting for perfection, one must learn to start where they are with what they have, gradually refining and adapting as they progress towards their life purpose—thus, start before you get ready. Life itself does not demand perfectionism; rather, it demands resilience, adaptability, and a willingness to embrace imperfection as an essential part of the journey towards fulfillment.

6. Need for acceptance.

The urge to seek approval from others, prioritizing external validation over internal aspirations, can steer individuals away from their life's purpose. When someone fixates on fitting in rather than standing out, driven by the desire to be liked and accepted by everyone, it can hinder their fulfillment. This constant need for acceptance breeds a cycle of comparison and competition, where individuals strive to outshine others to meet societal norms, neglecting their own visions in the process. This craving for approval stems from a deep-seated fear of judgment and rejection, discouraging individuals from pursuing their unique path towards fulfilling their life's purpose.

It is important to recognize that every vision begins with its own believer—the person who conceives it. If one fails to accept themselves and believe in their vision wholeheartedly, no one else will. In this journey towards self-acceptance, individuals must rely on their internal aspirations rather than seeking validation from external sources. It is imperative never to lose faith in oneself, as one ultimately becomes their own strongest supporter. In times of doubt or adversity, individuals must lean on their internal drive and determination, as they are their own ultimate backup.

By embracing their internal aspirations and trusting in their vision, individuals can break free from the shackles of societal expectations and chart their own unique path towards fulfillment. Instead of conforming to external standards, they can cultivate their passions and pursue their visions with unwavering confidence. This shift in mindset empowers individuals to embrace their selves authentically and live a life that resonates with their deepest desires.

7. Over or under perceived self-knowledge.

In the pursuit of self-understanding and becoming what you were destined to become by God, the Creator of all things, one may reach a point where they believe they have comprehensively grasped who they are. However, this conviction can lead to a dangerous state of being closed off to new experiences, feedback, and personal growth. Such an attitude fosters a rigid and overly confident mindset that obstructs the exploration of undiscovered aspects of oneself and inhibits necessary changes to align with one's life purpose. This phenomenon can aptly be termed as "over-perceived self-knowledge."

It is essential never to succumb to the delusion of being entirely self-sufficient and all-knowing, as this mindset blinds individuals to the valuable lessons that life seeks to impart. Arrogance, complacency, and a disregard for feedback are the pitfalls of overestimating one's understanding of oneself. These attitudes create subtle barriers to learning, adapting, and evolving in ways that are necessary for fulfilling one's life purpose.

Conversely, one should not allow their identity to be defined solely by external factors such as place of birth, educational background, family lineage, academic achievements, or past experiences. Self-awareness transcends these superficial labels. Instead, one's self-awareness, worth and commitment to living out their life purpose should outweigh the significance of these external influences.

It is very important to discern between the truth revealed by one's convictions and the illusions spawned by an inflated sense of self-knowledge. Blindly trusting in one's perceived understanding of oneself can prove more detrimental than remaining ignorant of one's true nature. It is necessary to remember that it is not the limitations one perceives within oneself that hinder progress, but rather the limitations one imposes upon oneself.

8. Comfort barriers.

The comfort barrier is when someone has become so accustomed to their routine or way of doing things that the mere thought of change scares them. They believe there is only one right way to do something and are hesitant to try anything new or untested. Instead, they follow the same path as everyone else, unaware that they have their own unique journey mapped out by God, the Creator of all things. It is important to realize that your path to fulfilling your purpose in life is distinct from anyone else's, so it is time to stop following in the footsteps of others if it not leading to your own path.

If you find yourself stuck in this mindset, the universe may intervene to push you onto your path, whether you are ready for it or not. This process is what I refer to as change; it is not something happening to you, but rather for you. While you may not understand the reasons behind every change, it is important to recognize that some changes can be incredibly painful and may leave you questioning the world around you.

The universe may expose you to experiences you have always tried to avoid and remove people from your life, all in an effort to shake you out of your comfort zone and propel you towards your passion. It is natural to feel overwhelmed by these changes, but it is crucial to secure your faith in God, the Creator of all things, and trust that everything is ultimately working in your favor.

However, it is important to acknowledge that not all changes are beneficial, which is why it is necessary to approach life with a healthy level of caution and maintain your faith in God, alone. By doing so, you can navigate through life's challenges with confidence, knowing that you are being guided towards your purpose.

9. Echoes of unresolved past trauma.

Freedom from the shackles of our past trauma is not attained until its influence on our future is severed. True liberation is achieved when one can openly discuss their past with a genuine smile, devoid of fear or apprehension regarding others' perceptions. The weight of secrecy and shame must be shed, for as long as we conceal our past transgressions, we remain imprisoned by them.

Each of us harbors a past we would rather keep hidden, yet when the need arises, confronting it openly is the key to dismantling its power. By publicly addressing the very topics others would use to gossip about us, we dismantle their ammunition. Secrecy breeds vulnerability; only by exposing our truths can we disarm those who would seek to use them against us.

Understanding how to confront and reconcile with our past is essential for safeguarding our future. Even some of history's most esteemed figures carried burdensome pasts, yet found redemption and renewal. The sacrificial act of Jesus Christ, in forgiving rather than reclaiming our past, serves to protect the future we are yet to live.

Paul of Tarsus, a key figure in the Bible who brought many people back to God, had a troubled past. He associated with murderers, and his reputation was widely known. Despite this, when God chose him to spread the Gospel of God's Kingdom, people still viewed him negatively. Some even tried to kill him, fearing he would harm those who lived Jesus Christ's life. However, Paul did not hide from his past. He acknowledged it openly, realizing that denying it would only hinder his future. When he appeared before King Agrippa for trial, he addressed his past honestly and publicly:

> *"My behavior and manner of living from my youth up is known by all the Jews; [they are aware] that from [its] commencement my youth was spent among my own race in Jerusalem. They have had knowledge of me for a long time, if they are willing to testify to it, that in accordance with the strictest sect of our religion I have lived as a Pharisee. And now I stand here on trial [to be judged on the ground] of the hope of that promise made to our forefathers by God, which hope [of the Messiah and the resurrection] our twelve tribes confidently expect to realize as they fervently worship [without ceasing] night and day. And for that hope, O king, I am accused by Jews and considered a criminal! Why is it thought incredible by any of you that God raises the dead? I myself indeed was [once] persuaded*

that it was my duty to do many things contrary to and in defiance of the name of Jesus of Nazareth. And that is what I did in Jerusalem; I [not only] locked up many of the [faithful] saints (holy ones) in prison by virtue of authority received from the chief priests, but when they were being condemned to death, I cast my vote against them. And frequently I punished them in all the synagogues to make them blaspheme; and in my bitter fury against them, I harassed (troubled, molested, persecuted) and pursued them even to foreign cities. Thus engaged I proceeded to Damascus with the authority and orders of the chief priests, when on the road at midday, O king, I saw a light from heaven surpassing the brightness of the sun, flashing about me and those who were traveling with me. And when we had all fallen to the ground, I heard a voice in the Hebrew tongue saying to me, Saul, Saul, why do you continue to persecute Me [to harass and trouble and molest Me]? It is dangerous and turns out badly for you to keep kicking against the goads [to keep offering vain and perilous resistance]. And I said, Who are You, Lord? And the Lord said, I am Jesus, Whom you are persecuting. But arise and stand upon your feet; for I have appeared to you for this purpose, that I might appoint you to serve as [My] minister and to bear witness both to what you have seen of Me and to that in which I will appear to you, choosing you out [selecting you for Myself] and delivering you from among this [Jewish] people and the Gentiles to whom I am sending you to open their eyes that they may turn

*from darkness to light and from the power of Satan
to God, so that they may thus receive forgiveness and
release from their sins and a place and portion among
those who are consecrated and purified by faith in Me"
(Acts 26:4-18).*

My dear friend, if ever the time comes for you to confront your
past, do so openly and honestly. If you shy away from it, the
embarrassment of your past actions will outpace the success
you hope for in the future.

10. Health (spiritual, soulical, and physical) issues.

Not being thrown off from living ones life's purpose, requires
the cultivation of three essential forms of wealth: spiritual,
soulical, and physical. Should any of these forms of wealth be
lacking, one's existence is immediately jeopardized, and this
reality must not be underestimated.

The first and foremost form of wealth to attain is not material
wealth, but spiritual wealth. This may seem counterintuitive to
some, but it is important to understand that as beings of spirit,
our primary focus should be on nurturing our spiritual selves.
This entails developing a deep faith in the God, the Creator
of all things, grounding our beliefs in God rather than solely
in His creations. Without such a faith, we become susceptible
to surrendering ourselves to the influences of the world,
forgetting that our true battle is not against flesh and blood,
but against spiritual forces of darkness, as stated in Ephesians
6:12. To be spiritually wealthy means to possess a steadfast
faith in God, nurtured through constant communication and

prayer, allowing God's Word to direct our paths, freeing us from sin.

The second form of wealth, soulical wealth, pertains to the health and strength of our minds. Our minds serve as the dwelling place for our consciousness, shaping the entirety of our existence. Therefore, it is imperative to safeguard our minds by being mindful of what we allow into them. Continuous learning, forgiveness, and the ability to let go of past hurts are essential for maintaining soulical wealth. Additionally, clarity of thought is achieved through the practice of seeking understanding rather than assuming, thereby fostering mental freedom from destructive anger.

Lastly, physical wealth encompasses the well-being of our bodies. A healthy body is essential for fulfilling one's purpose and enjoying the fruits of life. Engaging in regular exercise, prioritizing healthcare, maintaining a balanced diet, and presenting oneself in a manner befitting of respect are all integral aspects of physical wealth. After all, what good is amassed wealth if one's health is compromised, rendering them unable to enjoy it?

In effect, the ultimate project we should undertake in life is the cultivation of ourselves. By prioritizing spiritual, soulical, and physical wealth, we equip ourselves to live meaningfully and face death without regret. Each form of wealth complements the others, forming a foundation upon which a fulfilling life is built. Therefore, let us not neglect any aspect of wealth, but rather strive to attain balance and wholeness in all areas of our existence, so that we would not been thrown off from our life's purpose.

11. Trending addiction.

In our pursuit of staying relevant in living out our life's purpose, many of us constantly seek to stay abreast of the latest trends, fearing to be perceived as outdated amidst life's ongoing transitions. We go to great lengths to remain current, even immersing ourselves in these changes to garner attention or perhaps even create our own shifts in hopes of capturing the world's spotlight. At times, this drive leads us to engage in foolish actions, driven by a deep desire for recognition and validation. It is not uncommon for individuals to go to extreme lengths, such as exposing themselves on camera or adopting activism merely for show, all in pursuit of virality and acclaim. We do this to feel significant, to assert our presence in the world.

While this pursuit may seem appealing, it carries the risk of diverting us from our life's purpose, luring us into a vortex where we prioritize popularity over integrity. However, my friend, when we align ourselves with our life's purpose, recognition naturally follows, even in the most obscure corners of existence. People are drawn to authenticity, and they are willing to support those who live authentically. You will be astonished by how your purpose resonates with others, even those you have never met.

Yet, my friend, we must not become ensnared by the allure of fleeting trends without considering their long-term consequences, especially on future generations. There is no such thing as a private or inconsequential action; every choice we make has ripple effects, impacting both ourselves and those around us. Before succumbing to the allure of a trend, we must ask ourselves: Is it worthy of remembrance? Is it something we would want to pass on to future generations as a legacy? Is it aligned with our life's purpose, and does it contribute to making the world a better place?

We must remember that our actions should be grounded in our life's purpose, and that purpose should strive to leave a positive imprint on the world. Trending for the sake of trending is hollow if it lacks meaning and substance. Instead, let us ensure that our endeavors are meaningful, guided by a sense of purpose and a commitment to leaving the world better than we found it.

Chapter 7: Principles To Think About Before You Take Your Last Breath

———

1. The greatest personal revelation in life is that while your purpose is chosen by God, the Creator of all things, the ultimate fulfillment of that purpose rests squarely upon your own will power.

2. The ramifications of neglecting our life purpose are manifold and far-reaching. When individuals prioritize being more important over authentic fulfillment, the fabric of society begins to fray. Economic instability, social unrest, and geopolitical tensions are symptomatic of this deeper malaise—a collective disconnection from our inherent purpose and the values that underpin it.

3. Nothing catches God, the Creator of all things, as a surprise.

4. With our willpower, we can even refuse to be what we were born to be, reject the existence of God entirely, dismissing the notion of absolute morality and purpose in life.

5. You are not just a random mix of sperm and egg. Your existence on Earth is not a coincidence; it is part of a grand plan. The Earth needs you so much that your presence is important for the world to function properly. You are not a mistake of biology; no one on

this planet is. Your birth serves a purpose, a purpose set by God, the Creator of all things, and your purpose is unchanging and essential, even if life's challenges make it hard to believe.

6. Your journey may be tough, surrounded by people who do not understand or appreciate you. But as long as you stay true to yourself, your purpose will guide you through.

7. Never let your passion outrun your patience in God. Stay patient and trust in the timing of your purpose.

8. Even when you feel used or unappreciated, hold onto your purpose with pride. You have survived difficult times and persevered through misunderstandings, never losing sight of your true calling. Your purpose is your strength, a constant presence in a world of change.

9. Never forget that you are here for a reason, and that reason is something to be cherished and celebrated.

10. Parenthood does not equate to ownership of your child's life, nor does it confer omniscience regarding their destiny. It is imperative to listen to your children, cultivate intimacy to understand their capabilities, and seek God's guidance to figure out their life's purpose. Presuming to know what is best for them based on your experiences or others' is fallacious. Allow your children to feel secure in their own existence. Do not let your past traumas dictate their future. Your role is to nurture their journey towards re-discovering and fulfilling their life's purpose, ensuring they do not stray onto paths dictated by

others.

11. Deep within us lies the potential to change the world, but too often, we bury it under layers of societal conditioning. We are taught to suppress our inner voices, to never push back, to simply go along with the status quo. They feed us words like "cooperate" and "be submissive," all while secretly aiming to stifle our potential. We are like oxen, harnessed and controlled by threats, intimidation, and false promises of power. They instill fear to keep us in line, warning of pain if we dare to step out of bounds. But I believe that as you read this, you will cast off those chains and reclaim your sense of conviction and self-determination.

12. Let the conviction within you about yourself outweigh any doubts others may have about you. It is time to reclaim your passion and prioritize your own opinion of yourself over the judgments of others.

13. Do not become overly concerned or troubled if your purpose resembles that of someone else; what truly matters is how you execute it. It is natural to feel intimidated when you see others whose purposes seem similar to yours achieving great success, overshadowing your own emerging efforts. However, it is crucial to remember that while the objective may be similar, the method intended for you by God, the Creator of all things, is unique to you. Keep this thought firmly rooted in your mind to avoid doubting your abilities, skills, or the potential impact of your accomplishments on the world.

14. Avoid persistently fearing being perceived as

incompetent simply because you have not yet attained the level of success you desire. Do not let the fear of failure or inadequacy hold you back from taking risks and seizing opportunities for growth. Refrain from attributing your achievements or potential achievements solely to luck, chance, or external factors, without acknowledging the effort and determination you have put in. Success ultimately hinges on your effort and belief in yourself, so let your conviction about your abilities outweigh any doubts others may have about you. Unless if it turns other way round, you will submit to what the naysayers and the experts says.

15. Fear-based mindset stifles innovation and creativity, as individuals become more concerned with avoiding mistakes than seizing opportunities for progress towards their life purpose.

16. Life itself does not demand perfectionism; rather, it demands resilience, adaptability, and a willingness to embrace imperfection as an essential part of the journey towards fulfillment.

17. Every vision begins with its own believer—the person who conceives it. If one fails to accept themselves and believe in their vision wholeheartedly, no one else will.

18. It is necessary to remember that it is not the limitations one perceives within oneself that hinder progress, but rather the limitations one imposes upon oneself.

19. If you find yourself stuck in this mindset, the universe may intervene to push you onto your path, whether

you are ready for it or not. This process is what I refer to as change; it is not something happening to you, but rather for you.

20. Freedom from the shackles of our past trauma is not attained until its influence on our future is severed. True liberation is achieved when one can openly discuss their past with a genuine smile, devoid of fear or apprehension regarding others' perceptions. The weight of secrecy and shame must be shed, for as long as we conceal our past transgressions, we remain imprisoned by them.

21. Each of us harbors a past we would rather keep hidden, yet when the need arises, confronting it openly is the key to dismantling its power. By publicly addressing the very topics others would use to gossip about us, we dismantle their ammunition. Secrecy breeds vulnerability; only by exposing our truths can we disarm those who would seek to use them against us.

22. If ever the time comes for you to confront your past, do so openly and honestly. If you shy away from it, the embarrassment of your past actions will outpace the success you hope for in the future.

23. The first and foremost form of wealth to attain is not material wealth, but spiritual wealth. This may seem counterintuitive to some, but it is important to understand that as beings of spirit, our primary focus should be on nurturing our spiritual selves. This entails developing a deep faith in the God, the Creator of all things, grounding our beliefs in God

rather than solely in His creations. Without such a faith, we become susceptible to surrendering ourselves to the influences of the world, forgetting that our true battle is not against flesh and blood, but against spiritual forces of darkness.

24. Clarity of thought is achieved through the practice of seeking understanding rather than assuming, thereby fostering mental freedom from destructive anger.

25. People are drawn to authenticity, and they are willing to support those who live authentically.

CHAPTER

8

Living Effectively, Dying Satisfactory

———

T he biggest hidden truth throughout history is that deep down, everyone on Earth is searching for a key simple solution to live an easier life; to hit it further, to live an effective life and welcome death anytime without any sense of regrets of the need to live back again. Many people wrongly believe that the answer must be complicated, but in reality, it is straightforward and easy to miss because it is not complex enough to grasp. As a result, we often overlook it. We need to be aware that our time on Earth is limited, so we should not abuse it holding onto these false assumptions. We must stop experimenting and start living our life's purpose—thus, the key simple solution. This is not a semantic dilution.

Your life's purpose chooses your social circles, habits, priorities, time management, energy allocation, hobbies, reading materials, entertainment preferences, social engagements, leisure activities, dietary habits, financial decisions, values, attitude towards life, to-do list, and overall life plan. Essentially, it influences every aspect of your existence. Knowing your life's purpose is akin to having a roadmap for living, allowing you to embrace the present while keeping an eye on the future. This clarity empowers you to expect more from the world you envision within you, take courageous leaps of faith, and pursue aspirations beyond self-interest.

Consequently, living with purpose leads to a more focused and simplified life.

Re-capturing your life's purpose enables you to discern which choices align with your intended path and which ones do not. It provides a clear filter through which to evaluate opportunities, making it easier to decline those that do not serve your ultimate goals. Without a defined purpose, it becomes challenging to turn down opportunities that may lead you astray.

In effect, it is coming to the ultimate realization that your entire life on this planet Earth is a journey from the womb to the tomb, and that you are the one responsible for creating the path between the two that you desire to take in living out your life's purpose, ensuring that you do not miss fulfillment in every moment of your life.

God's scheme for GUIDINg the FULFILMENT of your life's purpose

I am certain that God, the Creator of all things, does not think you are serious about finding fulfilment in your life until He sees your plan for your life's purpose. Planning shows your faith in God. If God tells you something and you do not plan to do it, then you do not truly believe it. Planning is how you put God's vision for your life into action. Jesus Christ, our Lord and Savior, emphasizes the importance of planning our lives according to our purpose and gives us a scheme to guide us attain fulfilment all the days of our lives even as we follow Him, as stated below:

*"And anyone who does not **carry his cross and follow Me** cannot be my disciple. Suppose one of you wants to build a tower. Will he not **first sit down** and **estimate the cost** to see if he has enough money to complete it? For if he lays the foundation and is not able to **finish it**, everyone who sees it will ridicule him, saying, 'This fellow began to build and was not able to finish.' Or suppose a king is about to go to war against another king. Will he not **first sit down** and **consider** whether he is able with ten thousand men to oppose the one coming against him with twenty thousand? If he is not able, he will send a **delegation** while the other is still a long way off and will ask for terms of peace. In the same way, any of you who does not **give up everything** he has cannot be My disciple" (Luke 14:27-33).*

1. Carry his (your) cross and follow Me (God)— You are responsible for planning your life's purpose.

God is saying that because He is the one who provides vision, He believes in the vision He gives you, and it is best for you to turn that vision into reality. However, it is also up to you to believe in it, because you cannot achieve what you do not believe in.

Furthermore, God is emphasizing that the vision you see in your mind's eye is something you have not done before. You are like a virgin, and you need to follow Him through with determination to get it done. You should approach Him with a level of fear, so you can get it done, because you are not smart enough to figure out how your life's purpose is going to be accomplished.

God also wants you to understand that you are responsible for planning your life's purpose. He clarifies that the success of the vision you see in your mind's eye does not solely depend on you; it depends on Him. Your plans encapsulates your vision, as envisioned in your mind's eye.

The most crucial aspect, according to God, is that He only supports plans that are followed up with action. All plans requires effort, and the reason why some people fail to achieve their encapsulated visions might be due to a lack of action. Indeed, planning without action leads to failure.

God's perspective is clear: the success of your plan is not solely your responsibility. He takes on the responsibility of ensuring your success. Therefore, you should not hesitate to write down your plans. Do not worry about how they will succeed, as God assures that He will ensure their success. Simply entrust your plans to Him, and He will ensure they come to completion.

2. First sit down—Have a meeting with yourself first before meeting anyone else.

Let me offer you a word of caution: before engaging with others, it is essential to first sit down and have a meeting with yourself. This means deeply reflecting on what you believe you are meant to do in life, and letting that belief outweigh others' beliefs. If you share your vision with those who are more experienced and capable of supporting you, but they end up overshadowing your conviction with their own, they might unintentionally hinder your progress. These individuals, though well-meaning, can be deceptive, leading you astray with seemingly wise advice that subtly undermines your vision. It is necessary to be cautious and avoid such people to safeguard your vision.

The Bible wisely states, *"He who hates pretends with his lips, but stores up deceit within himself" (Proverbs 26:24).* Here, "deceit" refers to harboring intentions to hinder or harm another. Some of the wonderful people you may know may present themselves as allies, offering positive encouragement, while secretly harboring alternative motives that could lead you astray. Therefore, it is imperative to exercise discernment and caution when seeking assistance in pursuing your vision.

It is natural to seek guidance and support from others, particularly those who appear to have valuable experience and insights. However, many of such individuals may harbor insecurities and perceive your vision as a threat to their own achievements. Consequently, rushing into alliances with such individuals could inadvertently jeopardize the realization of your visions.

In effect, anchor yourself in your own conviction and surrounding yourself with genuine allies, you can safeguard your vision from potential derailment and confidently pursue your visions. Remember, the most crucial meeting you will ever have is the one you have with yourself.

3. Estimate the cost, or consider (the consequences)—Expected requirements and necessities.

Your purpose is what you truly enjoy doing, something you feel happy to pursue. It is what brings you joy every day, like a play day, and provides inner peace while helping you overcome traumas. However, it is possible that you maybe currently engaged in something that causes you stress and unhappiness, possibly even leading to your demise. This could be your job, a college program, or training sessions that you despise. Yet, to attain what you love, you must first endure what you dislike; this is akin to what God calls estimating the cost or considering the consequences..

You might be thinking about leaving your job because it is draining you, but have you really thought about what might happen if you do not find another well-paying job or if you are out of work for the next six years? Similarly, you might be considering dropping out of school because you have found something else you want to pursue, but have you stopped to think about why you originally chose that program? While it might feel like this training class is taking up a lot of your time and energy unnecessarily, have you considered the long-term benefits it might bring after completing the final session? If you are thinking about taking out a loan to fund your vision, have you explored other options or are you sure this is the best choice for you?

God, the Creator of all things, bestowed upon humanity a crucial gift: the ability to think and plan for the future. He gave us minds so that we could actively shape our destinies because the future is inevitable—it is unfolding anyhow, and our involvement in shaping it is essential. In Jeremiah 29:11, God promises a future for each of us, but He expects us to play a role in its creation, hence why He granted us minds. Allowing the future to unfold without active participation is a disservice because we are fully responsible for the experiences we wish to have. Therefore, it is vital to be prepared for every stage of our unfolding futures.

To pursue what you love, you must first estimate the resources and efforts required to fulfill your purpose successfully. This involves determining the time needed to master your craft, acquiring necessary knowledge and skills, and enduring unpleasant situations, such as a low-paying job, to finance your vision. It also entails cultivating relationships and committing to self-improvement through disciplined efforts.

The essence of this process lies in understanding your needs and what is expected of you to achieve your visions. This includes acquiring knowledge, skills, and resources necessary for your journey of becoming yourself and fulfilling your purpose.

4. Delegation—Knowing when to hand over tasks and when to go along with others.

In our previous discussion, we explored that purpose is interrelated, which God, the Creator of all things, designed to embody both dependence and independence. This purpose intertwines with the purposes of others, shaping the fabric of our lives. Understanding this concept can alleviate a great deal of stress. It is important to recognize that God reveals our purpose gradually, rather than all at once, through visions in our minds. If the full extent of our purpose were revealed immediately, we might doubt its authenticity, believing it was intended for someone else. Instead, God unveils our purpose in stages, allowing us to absorb and adapt to each revelation before moving on to the next. Although subsequent phases may seem daunting, they serve to refine our understanding and strip away preconceptions, preparing us for what lies ahead.

Whatever purpose God has assigned to us on Earth, it is intrinsically linked to our interactions with others. Our reliance on fellow humans is a fundamental aspect of God's design, enabling us to fulfill our purpose collectively. There will come times when God humbles us, leading us to seek assistance from individuals whom we may have previously overlooked. These individuals may lack formal education or seem outdated in their thinking, yet they possess invaluable insights and support vital to our journey.

Moreover, there are phases of our purpose that we cannot navigate alone; we must collaborate with others and utilize their resources to succeed. Recognizing the phase we are in is essential for progress. Additionally, God may guide us to delegate certain tasks and responsibilities to others, passing on our knowledge and skills to future generations. It is God's intention that the purpose He has instilled in us continues beyond our own lifetimes, ensuring its legacy endures.

Therefore, understanding the phase of our life's purpose is paramount. It enables us to embrace dependence on others, navigate collaborative efforts, and prepare for the transition of responsibilities. By embracing these principles, we can fully engage with our purpose and contribute to its enduring impact on the world.

5. Finish it, or give up everything—Is it worth sacrificing your entire life on this planet Earth for its completion?

To take control of living out your life's purpose, you need to let go of certain wonderful things and certain amazing people if they are not contributing to your journey. It should not take your whole life to understand that your life's purpose is something you must pursue for yourself, even before others can offer assistance. This means leaving behind distractions and focusing on what lies ahead. Sometimes if you are not willing to sacrifice something of value, you will never fully realize and experience your life's purpose. You can only achieve it by relinquishing something important to you, whether it is a habit, a relationship, a job, or even your comfort zone. Achieving your purpose means divorcing yourself from what no longer serves you, leaving it behind without looking back. This may seem extreme, but it is necessary to fully commit to your life's purpose.

Many people struggle to live their life's purpose because they keep returning to the things they should have left behind. It is essential to reach a point where you are willing to let go of even the most valuable distractions. You must internalize the belief that nothing is more important than fulfilling your life's purpose. Otherwise, you will never have complete control over your purpose.

It is crucial not to overestimate your current level of fulfillment and underestimate how much more you could achieve by letting go of what holds you back. Even if you think you are content with where you are, there is always room for growth and expansion. God challenges us to realize that our potential is far greater than we might imagine.

You must understand that you must fulfill your life's purpose before you take your final breath, or else you will have regrets when it is about time to enter the graveyard. Life is about completing the purpose you were born to accomplish before you reach the end. It is worth dedicating your entire life to this pursuit, as it is the most meaningful investment you can make.

The principal components in planning to live out your life's purpose completely and experience fulfilment until your last breath on this planet Earth

The plan for your life needs certain principal components. These bits make sure your plan is clear, easy to measure, has deadlines, reflective, can be adjusted, is doable, fits with what is going on around you, makes you distinct, and moves you forward. You should include these principal components as you go through life:

- **The principle of faith.**

The most important thing God wants from you is faith. Whatever you believe in, that is what God gives you. Your achievements in life depend on how much faith you have. If you believe you can achieve something, you can. Hold onto your faith. Never throw away your faith! Believe in God, take your daily relationship with God very seriously, and I repeat very seriously, and you will succeed. Just keep believing and take action, Heaven is backing you up.

- **The principle of becoming rare.**

Always invest in yourself and strive to be valuable rather than merely important. Aim to be so unique that you are the first choice when the world needs something done. God created you to stand out among the countless people on Earth, with a purpose that sets you apart. Master your talents, maximize your strengths (what you are best at doing) and fulfill your purpose to ensure you are always the one people turn to. If you do not showcase yourself, you will be overlooked, and your legacy may only be a tombstone. Focus on adding value in your area of expertise and use it to improve the world.

- **The principle of priority.**

To really make the most of your life and accomplished your life's purpose, you need to focus on what is important and use your time wisely. It does not matter how old you are or what stage of life you are in, what matters is understanding the times you are need, what you ought to do and getting started on it. You do not need to wait until you are older or have certain achievements before pursuing what you love or making a difference. Start with what you have and who you are, prioritize what is most important to you, and make use of the resources available to you.

- **The principle of character.**

If you are going to fulfill your life's purpose, you need to develop strong character and avoid compromise. You must believe that you are greater than your failures, more powerful than your weaknesses, and stronger than the negative opinions others may have of you. Additionally, remain humble, compassionate, and grateful, while holding onto your self-belief. Remember, you are valuable, and the world needs your purpose. Keep these thoughts in mind as you navigate life and remain disciplined. Never compromise your values by engaging in harmful behaviors such as promiscuity, substance abuse, or harming others. Always stay true to your convictions and prioritize honesty.

- **The principle of change.**

You need to be ready for things to change and adapt to them if you want to have fulfilment in your life. Expect good things, but be ready for bad ones to minimize feeling let down or sad. So, it is important to think about the changes you want in your life, because change is certain to happen whether you like it or not. Change is always happening and it is something you can count on. Nothing stays the same forever except change. Keep in mind that unexpected changes will happen, and you will need to adjust to them. Sometimes, life's purpose will require you to change your habits or goals because of the situation you are in, so do not be too strict with yourself about sticking to your plans. Your plans might change, but your life's purpose will always stay the same. You should always be ready to adapt to change because you cannot stop it. You can only decide whether to let it control you or to overcome it. I encourage you to overcome it by being proactive and dealing with the changes happening around you.

- **The principle of building a network of relationships.**

If you want to go further and make life easier, start making connections with people. Take the lead, be friendly, smile to attract others, and be open to them. Do not act like you are the only serious person in life or walk past others with pride, thinking they should approach you first. Everyone is equal, so kill your pride and politely reach out to others. Some of the people you pass may have the resources you need to fulfill your life's purpose. Remember, the cheerful smile on your face is not for you—it is meant to be shared with others. Your success in fulfilling your life's purpose and finding fulfillment within yourself depends also on the relationships you build.

- **The principle of timeframe.**

To make the most of your time on Earth, it is essential to use it wisely and not abuse it. Be careful about what you invest your time in, and ensure it aligns with your life's purpose. To fulfill your life's purpose, it is important to be proactive and complete tasks ahead of schedule rather than procrastinating. Take control of your life and plan it according to your desires, rather than letting life dictate your path. By starting early and being proactive, you can progress towards the tail end of your life's purpose and experience fulfillment. Remember, your time is precious, and abusing it means losing a part of your life forever. Everything you do on this planet Earth should be time bound.

- **The principle of system.**

Always remember that you are in this world's system, but not of it. If you start believing that you are of this word's system, then when it fails, you will fail too. However, if you firmly believe that you are in the system but not of it, then even if the system collapses, it would not affect you. This idea was taught by Jesus Christ before He left this world. Understanding this allows you to set not only goals but also create your own systems by governing your thoughts, improving your skills to stand out, maximizing your potential, and seeking to solve problems. Do not settle for mediocrity and become dependent on a job or any position that is not allowing you to fulfill your life's purpose, as there will always be others competing for the same positions. Keep striving to improve yourself constantly.

- **The principle of health.**

Your health should be your top priority because it is your main wealth. Without it, you cannot carry on living as a human on Earth. Take it seriously by eating well, staying clean, exercising, and going for checkups when needed. Make sure to include these in your life plan as you pursue your purpose.

- **The principle of reflection.**

If you want to feel satisfied and live your life's purpose right to the end, you must regularly reflect on the goals of your plan—thus, evaluate and judge yourself constantly. Think about what has helped you and what has not, including people, experiences, environment and situations. Sometimes, you might need to distance yourself from certain people, things, relocate your yourself to a new environment to achieve your goals. If you do not reflect on your past, you will keep repeating the same patterns. So, ask yourself if you want to live the same life for the next fifty years or beyond. If not, change your plans and make them clearer, achievable, relevant, measurable, specific, and time-bound. You are the artist of the experiences you want to live.

Creating your life's path (plan) in line with your life's purpose

God, the Creator of all things, wants you to participate in the purpose He gave you birth to fulfill on this planet Earth. Although He has a life plan for you to fulfill your life's purpose, He does not plan for you. And this is very important to take note of all the days of your life. He gave you the capacity to be the creator of your own life's path or plan, as King Solomon expressed in these words: *"Many are the plans in a man's heart, but it is the LORD's purpose that prevails" (Proverbs 19:21).*

That means your life's plan belongs to you; you are responsible for designing or creating it, but the purpose belongs to the Lord our God. That also means you were not built with the capacity to create your own life's purpose; all that you could do is acknowledge it. You can choose to ignore it, but that does not invalidate it. It also means God's purpose for your life is more powerful and important than your plans. This means that if you do not plan according to God's purpose for your life, you would not attain fulfillment in life, and this is a natural law. God's purpose for your life will always prevail over any plans that do not match His purpose. That means you need no judgment from God; you will be depressed, frustrated, stressed out, life will continue to beat you down, and that is exactly the result of not creating your life's path or plan according to God's purpose for your life.

Proverbs 16:1 also says *"To man belong the plans of the heart, but from the LORD comes the reply of the tongue."* Again, this verse of scripture emphasizes our need to create or design our own life's path or plan. But it also says something critical; it says *"...but from the LORD comes the reply of the tongue,"* which means God is committed to investing in your life's plan. Whatever it may cost, He says He will pay for it, so do not be afraid as you put your plans on paper. Because it is the very thing God is waiting for, as stated in *Proverbs 16:3 "Commit to the LORD whatever you do, and your plans will succeed."* That means God will not be able to succeed in anything in your life if you do not give it to Him to work on. God does not only succeed your plans; the good news is He also exceeds your plans, as stated in Ephesians 3:20. That is why when planning your life's plan, it has to be as big as your deepest desire. The Bible uses the word "exceed" as "sure," as stated in Proverbs 16:9 *"A man's mind [heart] plans his way, but the Lord directs his steps and makes them sure."* That also means God only directs your life's path or plan, not your highest prayers, shouting, affirmations, conviction, or faith, but it is your plans because that is the greatest expression of them all.

In every aspect of life, it is crucial to prepare diligently because God, the Creator of all things, is watching over you. As stated in Proverbs 21:5 of the Bible, *"Careful planning puts you ahead in the long run; hurry and scurry puts you further behind."* This means that when you plan, you should focus on your life's purpose. Why? Because planning gives purpose clarity. It defines how you will utilize your time, energy, resources, and relationships. Planning involves mapping out the journey from your birth to your death. It is about setting strategic goals to propel you towards a defined purpose. Purpose holds greater significance than plans because it demands agreement. Your life's plan needs to broken down into specific, understandable, measurable, actionable, relevant, progressive, and effective goals. These goals should be reviewed daily for necessary adjustments – a process known as documenting.

Documenting can be done digitally or on paper, providing a tangible reminder that can be revisited and meditated upon daily until it becomes ingrained in your consciousness. Now, let the above principal components be infused into your documentation. While some minority of does not have to be written down, these principles should be etched into your mind until they become your second nature. Documenting your life's path may span numerous pages, but do not be amazed, or worried, or even afraid; it is your life you are putting on paper, so embrace the process.

And remember that when documenting, the principle does not have to be in order as stated below; do it according to your own preference, reflecting how you want your life's path or plan to look. Again, it is not necessarily a must to follow how I have cited the principles in order; all you need to do is read through them and document them in order of your priorities according to your own preference. However, sticking to how I have done it does not create any problems at all.

Now, begin documenting:

Section 1: Document your "principle of faith."

- How will you enhance your prayer routine, both in the morning and before bed, as well as throughout the day? How will you ensure your quiet time is effective and how long will you dedicate to it? What aspects of your spiritual life, in connection with God, do you need to focus on to become more attuned to the spiritual realm? How much time will you devote to spiritual development each day, and through what means – fasting, studying God's word, praying for family and yourself, interceding for those in need? Outline your goals for strengthening your daily relationship with God to foster spiritual growth.

Section 2: Document your "principle of becoming rare."

- What qualities do you need to develop within yourself to fulfill your life's purpose? These might be the qualities you admire in others, which reflect upon you. What skills do you need to learn? What are one or two things you need to master and become experts in? What information do you need to gather? This could include books to read, documentaries and videos to watch, research to embark on, and courses to take. List them in short form or phrases, ensuring clarity and precision.

Section 3: Document your "principle of priority."

- What are the key steps you need to take to advance to the next level, which are essential and cannot be avoided? What is the most crucial legacy you should create and leave behind at your current stage of life, using the resources and abilities you have? This legacy might be something you build later in life, regardless of your age, and what steps must you take to achieve it? What resources are available to you now that you can utilize to enhance the quality of human life?

Section 4: Document your "principle of character."

- What are the things you are never going to compromise on? Are you never going to let anyone make you feel inferior without your permission? Or are you going to discipline yourself so much that no one could discipline? Is it not violating your purity until marriage? Is it that you are going to make your secret life as authentic as your public life, thus being the same person when no one is around and the same person when everyone is around? Is it that you are going to consider everybody as your teacher so that you can learn from their ignorance, errors, and mistakes, thus having no regrets? Is it that you are not going to look down on anyone else or use anyone else for your personal interest and then make them useless? Is it that you are going to be faithful all the time, or are you going to let your conviction be bigger than abusing conscience with lottery, alcohol, sex, smoke, or chemicals? Is it that you are not going to sell out your identity for any redefined unnatural identity? Write out the things you will never violate and the things you will uphold in high esteem all the days of your life.

Section 5: Document your "principle of change."

- What are the things you desire to experience in your life, along with the things you do not want to happen, and the generations in your lineage? What mistakes do you not want to repeat, what habits do you wish not to be anchored to anymore? What are the things you need to give up forever and never even see the shadows of again? What are the things you need to change in your life right now because they are suppressing the person you are becoming or turning you into something else instead of what you desire, and also what are the very things you need to maintain in your life permanently?

Section 6: Document your "principle of building a network of relationships."

- Who are the people you need to get close to because they have what you need to fulfill your life's purpose? Who has a similar purpose to yours and could become your mentor so you can learn a lot from them? What exactly do you want to learn from them? What strong relationships do you need to establish so they can support you on a long run, and who specifically, ensuring they would not change you or take advantage of you as you go through life?

Section 7: Document your "principle of timeframe."

- All that you will document as the goals towards fulfilling your life's purpose, make sure they are specifically time-bound, whether in minutes, hours, years, or age. This is what makes your life plan more specific, measurable, actionable, relevant, progressive, and effective. Otherwise, it will simply be ink on a page, never manifesting what you sees in the eyes of your mind. Attach the age or age range you desire to attain them, and specify the minutes, hours, or years you need to invest to achieve them. Always ensure that the goals of your life plan are clear and aligned with your life's purpose.

Section 8: Document your "principle of system."

- What thing are you going to improve upon for

yourself within the course of your entire life here so that if someone had to think about something that reminded them of you, it would be that? What efforts and sacrifices are you going to put in place to master that, to become so good at it or in that area that people cannot ignore you?

Section 9: Document your "principle of health."

- What is your eating routine going to be? When will you have breakfast, lunch, and dinner to keep your body healthy? How will you manage your medical checkups and keep your body clean and fit? What goals are you setting to stay healthy, and how much are you budgeting for that?

Section 10: Document your "principle of reflection."

- How will you assess yourself? Will it be at the end of each period—monthly, quarterly, half-yearly, or yearly? What is your goal for evaluation? What measures are you implementing to consistently assess your actions and ensure you stay on track?

A WORD FOR YOU

Do not allow it to consume almost your entire lifetime on this planet Earth before realizing that life is fundamentally a do-it-yourself project. Simply re-discovering the meaning of existence or creating a path or plan aligned with God's intentions for your life is not sufficient. The most important aspect is committing your life's path or plan to the Lord our God, the Creator of all things. While this may not seem like a sophisticated sentence, it holds significant weight, as commitment requires profound internalization and demonstration, signifying a readiness to not only live for it but also to die for it and bear any cost necessary to make it a reality. This commitment has the potential to impact succeeding generations long after you have taken your last breath on this planet.

Chapter 8: Principles To Think About Before You Take Your Last Breath

———

1. The biggest hidden truth throughout history is that deep down, everyone on Earth is searching for a key simple solution to live an easier life; to hit it further, to live an effective life and welcome death anytime without any sense of regrets of the need to live back again. Many people wrongly believe that the answer must be complicated, but in reality, it is straightforward and easy to miss because it is not complex enough to grasp. As a result, we often overlook it. We need to be aware that our time on Earth is limited, so we should not abuse it holding onto these false assumptions. We must stop experimenting and start living our life's purpose—thus, the key simple solution. This is not a semantic dilution.

2. Planning shows your faith in God. If God tells you something and you do not plan to do it, then you do not truly believe it. Planning is how you put God's vision for your life into action.

3. You cannot achieve what you do not believe in.

4. All plans requires effort, and the reason why some people fail to achieve their encapsulated visions might be due to a lack of action. Indeed, planning without

action leads to failure.

5. Anchor yourself in your own conviction.

6. Remember, the most crucial meeting you will ever have is the one you have with yourself.

7. Your purpose is what you truly enjoy doing, something you feel happy to pursue. It is what brings you joy every day, like a play day, and provides inner peace while helping you overcome traumas.

8. To attain what you love, you must first endure what you dislike.

9. The future is inevitable—it is unfolding anyhow, and our involvement in shaping it is essential.

10. Many people struggle to live their life's purpose because they keep returning to the things they should have left behind. It is essential to reach a point where you are willing to let go of even the most valuable distractions. You must internalize the belief that nothing is more important than fulfilling your life's purpose. Otherwise, you will never have complete control over your purpose.

11. It is crucial not to overestimate your current level of fulfillment and underestimate how much more you could achieve by letting go of what holds you back. Even if you think you are content with where you are, there is always room for growth and expansion. God challenges us to realize that our potential is far greater than we might imagine.

12. You must understand that you must fulfill your life's purpose before you take your final breath, or else you will have regrets when it is about time to enter the

graveyard. Life is about completing the purpose you were born to accomplish before you reach the end. It is worth dedicating your entire life to this pursuit, as it is the most meaningful investment you can make.

13. The most important thing God wants from you is faith. Whatever you believe in, that is what God gives you. Your achievements in life depend on how much faith you have. If you believe you can achieve something, you can. Hold onto your faith. Never throw away your faith! Believe in God, take your daily relationship with God very seriously, and I repeat very seriously, and you will succeed. Just keep believing and take action, Heaven is backing you up.

14. Always invest in yourself and strive to be valuable rather than merely important. Aim to be so unique that you are the first choice when the world needs something done. God created you to stand out among the countless people on Earth, with a purpose that sets you apart. Master your talents, maximize your strengths (what you are best at doing) and fulfill your purpose to ensure you are always the one people turn to. If you do not showcase yourself, you will be overlooked, and your legacy may only be a tombstone. Focus on adding value in your area of expertise and use it to improve the world.

15. It does not matter how old you are or what stage of life you are in, what matters is understanding the times you are need, what you ought to do and getting started on it. You do not need to wait until you are older or have certain achievements before pursuing

what you love or making a difference. Start with what you have and who you are, prioritize what is most important to you, and make use of the resources available to you.

16. You must believe that you are greater than your failures, more powerful than your weaknesses, and stronger than the negative opinions others may have of you.

17. Expect good things, but be ready for bad ones to minimize feeling let down or sad.

18. Nothing stays the same forever except change. Keep in mind that unexpected changes will happen, and you will need to adjust to them.

19. If you want to go further and make life easier, start making connections with people. Take the lead, be friendly, smile to attract others, and be open to them. Do not act like you are the only serious person in life or walk past others with pride, thinking they should approach you first. Everyone is equal, so kill your pride and politely reach out to others. Some of the people you pass may have the resources you need to fulfill your life's purpose. Remember, the cheerful smile on your face is not for you—it is meant to be shared with others. Your success in fulfilling your life's purpose and finding fulfillment within yourself depends also on the relationships you build.

20. Your time is precious, and abusing it means losing a part of your life forever.

21. If you start believing that you are of this word's system, then when it fails, you will fail too. However,

if you firmly believe that you are in the system but not of it, then even if the system collapses, it would not affect you.

22. Your health should be your top priority because it is your main wealth. Without it, you cannot carry on living as a human on Earth. Take it seriously by eating well, staying clean, exercising, and going for checkups when needed.

23. If you do not reflect on your past, you will keep repeating the same patterns. So, ask yourself if you want to live the same life for the next fifty years or beyond. If not, change your plans and make them clearer, achievable, relevant, measurable, specific, and time-bound. You are the artist of the experiences you want to live.

24. God, the Creator of all things, wants you to participate in the purpose He gave you birth to fulfill on this planet Earth. Although He has a life plan for you to fulfill your life's purpose, He does not plan for you. And this is very important to take note of all the days of your life. He gave you the capacity to be the creator of your own life's path or plan.

25. Your life's plan belongs to you; you are responsible for designing or creating it, but the purpose belongs to the Lord our God.

Afterword

———

The Earth needs you to stay. The world needs you to bring your vision into reality. You matter to your generation and the succeeding ones. Destiny has turned its face towards you because you are closer to your graveyard than ever.

Are you going to disappoint the world by abandoning your vision into a pit of excuses, disappointments, failures, distracting pleasures, imprisonment, poor health, poverty, conformity, societal expectations, low school grades from years ago, or by transferring blame and responsibility to others, whether it be your father, mother, siblings, family relatives for their lack of support or their high spiritual or intellectual sophisticated criticism against your vision on why you could not make it happen? I dare you to outgrow all these because the power to make it happen does not lie in them; it lies within you.

Or maybe you are going to let it take your entire life for you to realize that your life on this planet Earth is bigger than any religious conviction. Your human conviction is what carries the weight of your life. You were not born just to have daily prayers, perform ritualistic practices, shout, dance, praise, worship, or hold steadfast to any religious beliefs and traditions, or maybe just to exist to go to a called Heaven. I tell you, friend, never reduce your entire life to that. Again, your life is bigger than just observing the moon, being at the pulpit, and performing ritualistic practices. Never let all these outpace your passion in life.

It is time to respond to the call of destiny now. It is time to live intentionally and effectively so that you can welcome death at any time when it comes because you cannot postpone death's appointment with you; you can delay it with spirituality or medicine, but you cannot stop it. You will sense it in your nostrils when it arrives.

It is time, friend. The start is always frightening, but starting before getting ready is half done, so be wise and start now.

It is my dream that you will rob your graveyard with the solutions trapped within you that were destined there by God to solve our problems before you take your last breath. It is my dream that you will never let your passion outrun God's timing for you so that you do not end up doing anything that will make our planet Earth and the world worse than before. It is my dream that you would not throw off your conviction in yourself and your faith in God when doubts, fears, trials, and threats emerge on your way towards fulfilling your life's purpose. It is my deepest dream that you will bring out every vision within you, hold on to your faith towards the end of your life, make the world better than before, and welcome death wholeheartedly with a smile, laughter, without any sense of regrets because it has nothing to take from you that God installed within you when you arrived on this planet, and as you feel it in your nostrils, you too, like Paul of Tarsus, will say, *"For I am already being poured out like a drink offering, and the time has come for my departure. I have fought the good fight, I have finished the race, I have kept the faith. Now there is in store for me the crown of righteousness, which the Lord, the righteous Judge, will award to me on that day—and not only to me but also to all who have longed for His appearing"* (2 Timothy 4:6-8), or like our Lord and Savior, Jesus Christ, *"It is finished"* (*John 19:30*).

Copyright

———

About The Author

———

Joseph Bekoe Mfoamfo, known by the pen name Paa Kwasi Mfoamfo, hails from a humble background in Larteh-Akuapem, Eastern region of Ghana, West Africa. Paa Kwasi Mfoamfo, an influential speaker, delves into fundamental issues that shape human conviction, encompassing spiritual and social dimensions. His teachings revolve around living effectively and dying satisfactory, while also addressing the prevailing moral and ethical challenges in our swiftly evolving global society. Paa Kwasi Mfoamfo's personal conviction aligns with a broader human perspective, and his vision for the world seeks to instigate positive change from a grounded, realistic, and sustainable standpoint – a place he refers to as Heaven.

Paa Kwasi Mfoamfo's impactful messages are imbued with power, serving to inspire, motivate, challenge, and empower individuals. His focus lies in prompting humanity to pause, look inward, and consider their values, choices, and impact on others and the world around them. To re-discover their true selves, unlock unused potentials, and actively contribute to their immediate surroundings and the wider global community. The ultimate goal is to encourage people to leave a lasting impact before they take their last breath on this planet Earth.

You are welcome to contact Paa Kwasi Mfoamfo directly at his personal email, **mfoamfo@gmail.com**, if you would like him to speak at your conference, anniversary, meeting, or to motivate your team. He is open to invitations from companies, organizations, associations, or any social clubs focused on enhancing the well-being of people.

Don't miss out!

Visit the website below and you can sign up to receive emails whenever Paa Kwasi Mfoamfo publishes a new book. There's no charge and no obligation.

https://books2read.com/r/B-A-QFMEB-ESLZC

BOOKS 2 READ

Connecting independent readers to independent writers.

Milton Keynes UK
Ingram Content Group UK Ltd.
UKHW020910220424
441551UK00017B/1105